Varenna Writers Club

# Expressions

Volume III

2014

*Unexpected Consequences*

Edited by Susan Bono

ISBN-13: 978-1503182653
ISBN-10: 1503182657


The Varenna Writers Club is sponsored by
Varenna at Fountaingrove.

Our brightest blazes of gladness are commonly kindled by unexpected sparks.

Samuel Johnson

# Contents


**Leona Biddle**

I Stand at the Door of Memory . . . . . . . . . . . . . . . . . . . 25

Mother Knows Best . . . . . . . . . . . . . . . . . . . . . . . . . 41

A Life-changing Decision . . . . . . . . . . . . . . . . . . . 73

The Gold Ring . . . . . . . . . . . . . . . . . . . . . . . . . 128

**Joyce Cass**

New Arrival . . . . . . . . . . . . . . . . . . . . . . . . . . 12

Neither a Borrower nor a Lender Be . . . . . . . . . . . . . 85

A Singular Sympatico Sunday . . . . . . . . . . . . . . . . . 119

Four Haiku . . . . . . . . . . . . . . . . . . . . . . . . . . 167

**Karin Fitzgerald**

The Dream . . . . . . . . . . . . . . . . . . . . . . . . . . . . 2

A Christmas Memory . . . . . . . . . . . . . . . . . . . . . . 39

Game On: Hurray for Hockey . . . . . . . . . . . . . . . . . 64

The Evolution of a Cook . . . . . . . . . . . . . . . . . . . 96

**Dorothy Herbert**

Unexpected Consequences . . . . . . . . . . . . . . . . . . . . 1

Clutter . . . . . . . . . . . . . . . . . . . . . . . . . . . . 76

Waiting and Patience . . . . . . . . . . . . . . . . . . . . 107

Question . . . . . . . . . . . . . . . . . . . . . . . . . . . 135

**Nancy Humphriss**

Shall We Dance? . . . . . . . . . . . . . . . . . . . . . . . . 19

A Hard Lesson Learned . . . . . . . . . . . . . . . . . . . . 35

Beware of What You Wish For . . . . . . . . . . . . . . . . . 77

My Bali Hai Experience . . . . . . . . . . . . . . . . . . . 161

**Shirley Johnson**

    The House on Taylor Road . . . . . . . . . . . . . . . . . . . . 13

    A Message and a Dream . . . . . . . . . . . . . . . . . . . . 49

    The Book with the Avocado Green Cover . . . . . . . . . 82

    Happiness . . . . . . . . . . . . . . . . . . . . . . . 168

**Nikki King**

    On Becoming an Artist . . . . . . . . . . . . . . . . . . . . 22

    Blind Date . . . . . . . . . . . . . . . . . . . . . . . 111

    Celebration . . . . . . . . . . . . . . . . . . . . . . . 125

**Judith Klausner**

    He . . . . . . . . . . . . . . . . . . . . . . . . . . . 24

    My Zadye's Alcove . . . . . . . . . . . . . . . . . . . . 52

    A Short Love Story . . . . . . . . . . . . . . . . . . . 121

    Mama Goes to the Bronx . . . . . . . . . . . . . . . . . 140

**Elisabeth Levy**

    Unexpected Consequences . . . . . . . . . . . . . . . . . . . 5

    A New Generation of Unexpected Consequences . . . 69

    Bibifax . . . . . . . . . . . . . . . . . . . . . . . . 116

    The Varenna Prune Saga . . . . . . . . . . . . . . . . . 154

**Hal Peters**

    My Smoking Days . . . . . . . . . . . . . . . . . . . . . 31

    For Worse or for Better . . . . . . . . . . . . . . . . . 90

    Four Crashes and You're Out . . . . . . . . . . . . . . 131

    Anyone for Pinochle? . . . . . . . . . . . . . . . . . . 151

**Jack Russ**

Her List . . . . . . . . . . . . . . . . . . . . . . . . . . . . . . . . . 58

A KWIKTAX Caper . . . . . . . . . . . . . . . . . . . . . . . . 86

Client Care . . . . . . . . . . . . . . . . . . . . . . . . . . . . . 136

**Bernice Schachter**

Visual Puns . . . . . . . . . . . . . . . . . . . . . . . . . . . . 108

**Floyd Schlosser**

Fish Don't Bite With Their Teeth . . . . . . . . . . . . . . 17

Surprise . . . . . . . . . . . . . . . . . . . . . . . . . . . . . . . . 57

**Sally Tilbury**

Grand Entrance . . . . . . . . . . . . . . . . . . . . . . . . . . 28

The Curtain Opened . . . . . . . . . . . . . . . . . . . . . . . 44

Dare to be a Bubble . . . . . . . . . . . . . . . . . . . . . . 112

Cleaning the Barn . . . . . . . . . . . . . . . . . . . . . . . . 156

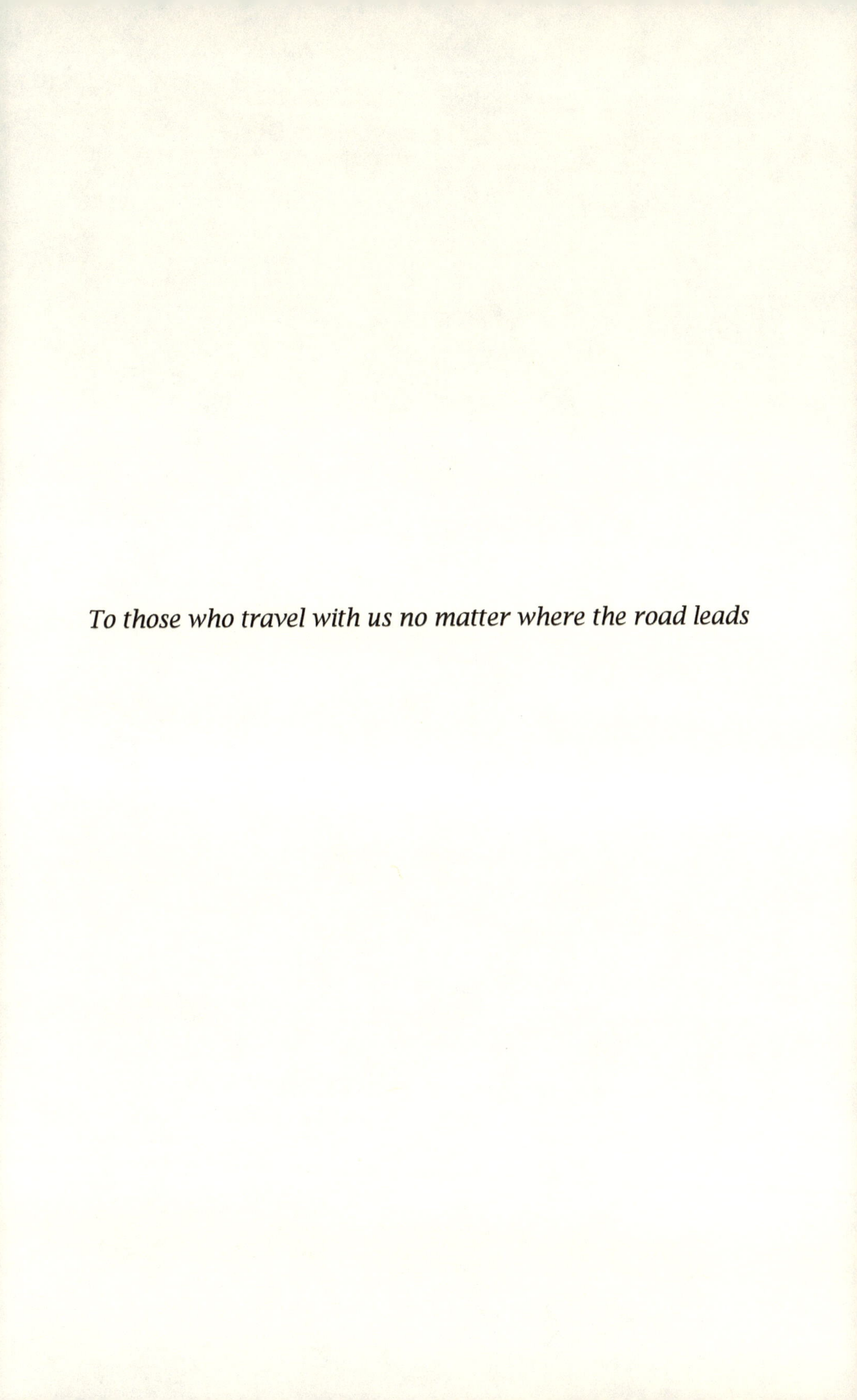

*To those who travel with us no matter where the road leads*

# Unexpected Consequences
## Dorothy Herbert

I was twelve years old when my beloved mother passed away after a long illness. She left behind a grieving husband and four young children. After a year or so, my father remarried a widow with three young daughters. Their ages intermixed with ours. So we went from a family of four to a family of seven children.

# The Dream
## Karin Fitzgerald

I always heed my dreams. Since the tragic drowning death of my dear eleven-year-old brother was eerily foretold in a full-color dream I had the night before, I view the occasional horrifying dream as a warning to me of coming events.

The ferry trip from Ketchikan, Alaska, to the capitol city of Juneau with my little toddler son holds no qualms for me. I eagerly look forward to being reunited with my husband, who is a young Assistant U.S. District Attorney. He has been assigned to several months work in Juneau trying cases. This assignment has presented some difficulties. We have to sublet our cozy apartment in Ketchikan and then sublet an apartment in Juneau. My husband and I choose to regard this as an adventure. I know from his phone calls that he misses us terribly.

We'll be on the ferry overnight and I feel certain that Dennis will like sleeping in a bunk bed. The cabin is comfortable, but once settled in, I take my nine-month-old son by the hand and we start exploring. We wander into the large main salon, and meet people who are surprised that such a small child could be walking so confidently. Dennis has been toddling around since he was seven-and-a-half months old. The only jarring note is a cry of outrage when a large swell makes the footing a little unstable and toddler Dennis lurches into a chess game, upsetting the board. The two old men scramble to pick up the pieces and the one who yelped shame-facedly apologizes and pats Dennis on the head. It's a mutual apology and I say that we're sorry and hope that they'll be able to continue their game.

After dinner, I carry my sleepy little boy to our cabin and read him his favorite story, then tuck him into the lower bunk. It has an ingenious extra piece that looks like the close-set bars on a crib. This side slides into place and is secured with a latch that the child can't reach. I'm impressed with the perfect simplicity of this arrangement. Tired now, I climb the few ladder-like stairs up to the top bunk and read for awhile. The shipboard lullaby hums me to sleep with the barely heard, steady, reassuring *Thrum, Thrum, Thrum* of the powerful engines and the faint sound of the waves whooshing against the prow of the ship as we head to Juneau.

Sometime during the night, the dream appears. I'm leaving the ship and have Dennis in my arms. As I step out toward the moveable gangway and take a step forward to start the short walk down to the dock below, the gangway separates from the deck. A gaping emptiness is before me where only a moment before the footing had been solid. I can see the water glinting and slapping against the piers below and feel Dennis slipping out of my arms. I wake up, heart pounding crazily and so frightened I clamber out of my bunk and stand looking down at my sleeping son, the most precious person in my universe. I'm afraid to go to sleep and sit up the rest of the night.

We dock in Juneau shortly after breakfast and I decide what I must do. The portent of the dream is as real as my life. I request that the officer who has been assigned to assist the passengers as they exit the ship hold onto me and I refuse to step out until he reluctantly places his hands on my shoulders. Dennis and I are the first ones off the ship. I have Dennis in a bear hug so tight that he starts to protest. As I lift my foot to take the first step, it's a real life horror story. The gangway starts to separate from the deck with a terrible grinding noise. The scream catches in my throat and strong hands yank us back to safety. I'm shaken and trembling, but try to collect myself, because I don't want to scare my darling boy. I hold him in my lap as repairs are made. I wait until all of the other passengers have exited uneventfully down the gangway. My husband is waving and smiling up at us and may wonder why one ship's officer is walking in front of us and one immediately behind as Dennis and I leave the ship.

I don't tell my husband about my dream until many years later. The heart-numbing terror of the dream and what happened the next day will never be forgotten. I always heed my dreams.

# Unexpected Consequences
### Elisabeth Levy

Shortly after the anthology, "Seasons," was published, our teacher began asking for stories about "unexpected consequences." I had to think long and hard until I realized I would not be here at Varenna without them. As I look back, my life was full of unexpected consequences and circumstances.

For example, at the age of nineteen I was ready to become a children's nurse. The Swiss School of Nursing had two programs, one for general nursing, a three-year program, and one for children's nursing, lasting two and a half years. I already had a serious boyfriend, planned to get married, start a family, and have lots of children. The woman who was my nanny until I was eight years old and my sister Erika already had their diplomas in general nursing. Both had convincing arguments as to why I should complete general nursing first and then specialize in children's care. They succeeded. I caved in and signed up for general nursing.

It was not so much their convincing arguments, however; it was my remembering that Erika started her training in the postpartum unit. (At that time the hospital stay for new mothers was ten days). Naïve as I was, I figured the same thing would happen to me. Reality hit hard. My first assignment was in a men's ward. Fortunately, we were a great group of girls supporting each other. The regimen was strict, conditions were harsh, and sometimes I wonder how we survived. The highlight for me was that, to the envy of my classmates, I received at least three love letters a week from my boyfriend.

Diploma in hand, I decided to spend the month of December at home and enjoy helping with the Christmas preparations. Another unexpected consequence happened. My father, a Protestant minister, was a member of the village council's division for social welfare. He was in charge of employing a new visiting nurse. When he learned this newest one had not disclosed her faith as Catholic, she was fired immediately. At that time our small village consisted mainly of Protestant citizens. There was no question, a visiting nurse in a community of under two thousand citizens was automatically involved in the well-being of everybody, hence the emphasis on the faith of each specific village. Who was asked to step in and help out? I did so grudgingly, but soon I began to enjoy it. I visited at least ten patients a day, and a few patients needed me for night duty as well. Besides that, I organized medical equipment, let the patients rent it for a minimal fee and kept tab, which had not been done before.

In the meantime, my boyfriend and I split up. Basically, I wanted to get married and he was not ready. The urge to take care of children surfaced again. How about taking a nanny job in England and improving my English?

I was recommended to a family with four children. I applied and was immediately rejected, a blow to my ego. They felt I was overqualified. Unexpectedly, I found a family with two girls and a third one on the way. It was a perfect match. To this day, we are still in touch. However, on the way to London, I spent a few days in Amersfoort, Holland, and fell in love with a Dutchman. I planned to work a few months in England and go back to Holland, except the love cooled off quickly.

While I worked in England, my father had a stroke and had to give up his ministry. I returned to Switzerland and wondered what was next on my agenda. My parents had moved and I applied for a job in a hospital close to their new home. During this time, my sister Erika had a job vaccinating people against tuberculosis. She had to travel from city to city on a moped, a motorized bicycle. Since our parents' new home had four bedrooms, Erika and I both stayed with them and were able to help our father through his last days.

Eventually, I became unhappy with working in the hospital, but once again, the unexpected happened. Erika told me a friend of hers was leaving her job in a dermatologist's office. She suggested I get in touch with her and find out what the position entailed. I did, and secured an interview with the dermatologists' wife. She approved of me, recommended me to her husband, and I was hired. After five years, I put my thinking cap on. If I stayed there, by the time I was fifty, my boss would turn sixty-five and retire. How would I land another job at that age?

About that time, a classmate of mine from nursing school showed up unexpectedly at our office. She had worked in San Francisco, returned for a vacation, and was on her way back to San Francisco. She asked me to join her across the ocean; it would be more fun to travel together. Erika had left Switzerland for the U.S. one year earlier. I had plans to find a job in Hong Kong, but under these new circumstances, I decided to change my plans and go to the U.S. as well.

The slowest ship we could find was the *Maasdam*, with the Holland America Lines. It took ten days from Southampton to New York. On the ship we found a bunch of other young people with as little money as we had. We laughed, had a good time, and even made fun out of being served the same potatoes every day under a different name.

Erika met us in New York. She had worked in Miami and had a Florida nursing license. Her car needed more oil than gasoline. Five of us, Erika, my friend Margaret, another Swiss girl, Agnes, and a Swiss man, Tommy, ventured out together. Within two weeks we were in Madison, Wisconsin, where Agnes's English-speaking relatives lived. Talk about language problems: Agnes phoned her aunt and thought she said, "Don't bring your friends," when in reality, she had dinner prepared for us and invited us to spend the night.

The next stop was in Salt Lake City. Margaret and Tommy, whose brother and family lived in Pacifica (called Sharp Park at that time), went directly to San Francisco. Erika and I decided to start our adventure in Portland, Oregon. With a shortage of nurses, finding a hospital job was no problem.

My first patient was a nine-year-old girl. When her family tried to avoid hitting a deer at night, their car crashed and caught fire, resulting in extensive burns for her and other family members. She subsequently died, the day before her tenth birthday.

While in Portland, I applied for an Oregon nursing license, only to find out I needed additional coursework in psychiatry. We had met two Danish nurses who decided to spend the winter months in Galveston, Texas. Without further ado, we packed up and drove to Texas.

Galveston was a third class seaport. We both worked in a private hospital, Erika in a medical ward for the indigents, I on a private floor. We never had encountered roaches before; here they were, and cheaper by the dozen. During an evening shift, Erika took a spray can to kill the roaches, only to find the dead ones in masses all over, in the water glasses, on the tables. A disaster, much worse than before.

After three months, we left Galveston, went on to San Antonio, and found a slightly better working situation. The roaches were still there, but not as numerous. I had applied for a Florida license and without ever having set foot on Florida soil, I got it.

After four months working in San Antonio, Erika decided it was time for her to move on to San Francisco. I just had met a young man, and we both showed interest in each other. It was a hard decision for me, but since Erika and I had only one car and very few earthly possessions, I finally figured it would be better to drive with Erika to San Francisco and return to San Antonio later. That never happened.

Now we were in San Francisco looking for jobs again. Erika ended up at Kaiser Permanente while I applied for a job at St. Mary's hospital, close to where we found an apartment. The interviewing nun shook her head as she read my resume: three months in Portland, three months in Galveston, four months in San Antonio. What were my plans now? Convincingly, I said I planned to stay in San Francisco. I did not tell her I really didn't like hospital work. After I got the job, I asked every physician I met at the hospital if he needed a nurse in his office and they all said they needed secretaries, not nurses.

Gradually I met more and different people. One was the husband of a friend of Erika's from Switzerland. He, a physician himself, suggested that I put an ad in the *San Francisco Medical Society Bulletin*, which I did: "Swiss nurse with five years' experience in Dermatology is seeking employment."

Two dermatologists responded, Dr. A and Dr. L. The first interview with Dr. A. went quite well. I was offered a certain monthly salary, and the way I understood it, this was his top offer. The second interview was slightly different. There were still patients in the waiting room when I arrived at the appointed time, and I was asked to wait. Dr. L. offered less money, but he promised after three months he would raise my salary if I proved myself and was doing my job well. I returned home and told Erika the outcome of the two interviews and that I had to make a decision now. Erika said,

"You already made your decision simply telling me the facts."
She was right. Neither physicians knew me, nor did they know
how it would work out. One gave me the chance to prove
myself, and I did.

One month later, he gave me the first raise, and many
moons later, he asked me to marry him. We worked hard, we
worked well together, and we had a good life together.

One sunny morning in April 2004, my husband opened
the *San Francisco Chronicle*. "Look at this ad for Varenna, a
new retirement place for independent living that will be built
in Santa Rosa. Let's go and check it out." And so we did.

We were #68 to sign up. We didn't mind waiting until it
was built. We still saw patients and kept the office going. We
attended scheduled dinners and met other prospective
residents until the unforeseen happened. Bill could not shake
his illness and died one year later.

The last unexpected consequence happened with me
breaking down completely. The opening of Varenna was
pushed out farther and farther, and living alone on our
beautiful hill in Marin became a nightmare. A phone call from
June M. asking me to check out Oakmont for renting a house
turned out to be my salvation. I found the right place, the
right friends who helped me adjust to my different life, and
finally Varenna opened its doors, and here I am to write
about it.

# New Arrival
## Joyce Cass

Oh, once there was a baby born

Her parents named her Polly

Expecting a boy

They howled with joy

Isn't she sweet; the family's complete

And so it was, by golly!

# The House on Taylor Road
## Shirley Johnson

When my children were very young, we bought four different houses, sold three as we moved around, lost a little money on all three, and for forty years lived in the fourth. It is the second house I want to write about, as it was certainly the most interesting, and, depending on your taste, the most charming, unusual, imaginative, and spooky. Spooky because of its history.

The construction materials were common enough in California, clear redwood, adobe brick, and lots of glass, but they were put together in a highly individual way. For one thing, there were no right angles in the rooms, and because the house had no hallways, both bedrooms, and even the one bathroom, opened directly off the large living-dining area that seemed spacious because of the high, open-beam ceilings. The bathroom was one step up from the living room, which made entrances and especially exits uncomfortably conspicuous, like stepping down from a stage. The sunken bath was a prize feature of the house, triangular in shape, made of Mexican tiles, and large enough for my three small children and one or two of their little friends to bathe together, to their great delight. The kitchen was a small pie-shaped area, dark and inconvenient, but brightened by a small eating room that had been clumsily added on, apparently as an afterthought. The single-wall construction and the big window gave it natural air-conditioning, and I could often see my breath there on winter mornings.

In spite of the drawbacks, we bought the house loving its uniqueness and ignoring its inconveniences at first. My husband hated the idea of being a suburbanite with a row house and lawn like everyone on the block, and this house certainly filled the uniqueness requirement. Its best feature was a sunny, pleasant back yard with a view to the hills of Carmel Valley, but the real reason we bought it was that it was the only house in Carmel in our price range. It had been hard to sell because of a violent, bloody and unsolved murder a few months before we arrived.

The victim was an ex-Hollywood starlet with a few pictures to her credit in years before, among them, a bit part in Al Jolson's "Jazz Singer" and another where she danced the tango with Rudolf Valentino. After being widowed and no longer getting casting calls, Clara Mohr left Hollywood for Carmel, where she designed and built the house on Taylor Road. She earned a living as a practical nurse, taking patients into her home. She was brutally attacked one stormy night and dragged into the bedroom, where she was again attacked and left to die. All that time, her elderly bedridden mother was in the next room. Strangely, she was unable or unwilling to give any help to the police.

Everyone on the street wanted to forget the murder,

and of course, I did, too. My next door neighbor, Edie, wouldn't come inside my door. Even when I called her from town asking her to see if I had turned off the stove, she still was so frightened she refused to go into the house. It was almost impossible to find a babysitter when we first moved there. As I later learned, my neighbor on the other side, Uvonna, was the one who found the murdered woman. Her husband, Markham, a realtor, was happy to have someone in the house again after it had been vacant for a few months, but he was jumpy, too. One night when I was alone because my husband was away on business, I awoke to see a flashlight moving in the back yard. It was Markham who thought he had heard noises and went to investigate, gun in hand. I did not find this reassuring.

Now I wonder that I was not more fearful to live in that house whose redwood beams creaked, making it sound like someone walking through the house. Later, the memory of the crime faded. We had two more children, and the pall that hung over the house largely disappeared. We sold it when we moved to Washington, D. C., and the realtor who listed it bought it and lived there for almost thirty years. I have lately found out that the house was razed in 2006 and a McMansion built in its place.

After we left Carmel and I was living in Rancho Murieta, I had a surprise visit from a detective who was sent by the Sheriff of Monterey County to question me about the murder and what I knew of the family that lived next door at the time. Their daughter, Markli, who was three when Clara

Mohr was murdered, now lived in northern California and was seeing a psychiatrist who practiced age regression, a therapeutic technique used to bring back memories of traumatic events, even from early childhood. Markli told the psychiatrist that the man who killed Clara was someone she had often seen in the house next door. This was reported to the Carmel police and confirmed what they had suspected at the time of the murder: that it was Clara's brother who often visited her and who finally murdered her. It explained why the mother would not give the police any information which would have implicated her own son. He no longer lived in California, and as the budget for the local police was tight and not adequate for an out-of-state investigation, they dropped the case. When the information was brought to the attention of the County Sheriff, they concluded that Clara's murderer was indeed her brother, now a very elderly man, and again the case was dropped.

The house is no more, no one I once knew still lives on Taylor Road, and my memories of that time are mostly happy ones. I didn't share the story of Clara Mohr with my children until it no longer had power to frighten them. It became just an interesting story of a place their parents bought and sold before finding another house on another road in Carmel, which became the place they called home until they left for college.

# Fish Don't Bite With Their Teeth
## Floyd Schlosser

No matter what boys decide to do or who is supposed to do the chores, chores are a bloody burden designed to destroy a boy's full life. In our case, a back-breaking chore of delivering one hundred and forty newspapers awaited us. Delivering them was a family project and there's nothing quite like a weekly newspaper route to cement family unity. The first three weeks of our new job, my brother was enamored, especially on collection day. The only problem was that the money wasn't ours to spend. What he collected would be spent as needed for the whole family.

What is it about a July afternoon that boys can't resist? This was a day to have fun, not deliver papers that carried five-day-old news that interfered with our fun. So the papers lay on the sidewalk in front of our house.

My brother Warren and I wanted to go swimming, so off to the lake we ran. The old swimming hole was half sandy bottom and half dirty mud. We slid into the water and began our routine of splashing and trying to grab our kicking legs out from under each other. As we water-wrestled, my brother accidentally clipped me on my chin and my two front false teeth popped out. (A year previously, I had fallen off a carrot truck and the brick road smashed my nose.)

I was petrified, but not Warren. As I wailed at my loss, he began diving to the muddy bottom to rescue my teeth. On the second dive, he found them and yelled, "Fish don't need your teeth!"

"I need them or my ass is grass," I laughed.

As we approached our house, Mom was out front examining two stacks of newspapers we hadn't delivered. I turned my head away as I tried to slip past her. Too late. She'd already seen my smashed-in mouth without my teeth. I could see she was about to blow a gasket.

I reached up, waving my mud-covered teeth as if it explained everything. It didn't. She followed me inside.

"Floyd, what in the world are you going to do next?"

She smiled, almost laughed.

Wow, I was safe.

"Wash up," she said. "Don't rub too hard. So, boys, it's time to deliver newspapers, and Floyd, for goodness sake! Don't smash anyone's windows."

# Shall We Dance?
## Nancy Humphriss

When Emily, newly widowed, moved to Varenna, our independent living community, in March of 2010, she had no trouble integrating into the community. She was eager to find out what events, committees, social activities, exercise classes, and games would interest her, and she participated in many things on an experimental basis. After a month or so, she had selected several of those best suited, and had also made friends with whom she socialized.

One day, another resident invited Emily to go to the Finley Center to a dance. Although she had not in her past life been much of a ballroom dancing enthusiast, the idea of going out and having a fun evening appealed to her. After a few minutes of stepping on her partner's toes, she realized she knew nothing at all about dancing. At this point, someone advised her to attend some beginning dance lessons! There she observed people of all ages involved with each other, swaying or swinging with the music, obviously greatly enjoying themselves. The scene before her stimulated something inside her and this something took hold and grew. As Emily said, "It was as if a light had suddenly gone on."

A new Arthur Murray Studio had opened in January of 2013 on Davis St. in Railroad Square, Santa Rosa. So in March 2013, after checking out the details of the studio, Emily decided to go alone for the free first dance lesson. The experience totally captivated Emily, and, without hesitation, she signed up for twelve individual lessons, which included two pairs of dance shoes. Actually, the dance shoes sealed the deal! Her two daughters, when she told them the details, were at first surprised. But after listening to their mother extoll her newfound joy, they quickly changed their minds and became totally on board.

Her instructor, a handsome, elegant, graceful young man of twenty-three, made her feel comfortable and accepted right away. He is a full time teacher, having gone through extensive training, not only in the practical methods of doing the dance steps, but also in the psychology of teaching dance: how to relate and understand his student, how to explain and recognize what she needs, using both verbal and visual examples. As a result, Emily has a feeling of friendship, trust, confidence, and joy as she glides across the floor with Zach. Emily now goes twice a week for her private lessons as well as three or four times a week for group lessons.

The dance program is set up in levels, with four parts to each level. The difficulty of these is somewhat like the Olympic medals: bronze, silver, and gold. Each level takes six months to a year to complete with six dance styles to master: smooth style being waltz, fox trot, and tango; rhythm style being cha-cha, rumba, and swing. After each level is

20

completed, there is a special "graduation" event, where friends and family are invited to come and witness the accomplishments achieved. Dale and I were lucky enough to have been asked to go to her bronze level event, and we were delighted to see Emily doing her quite amazing dances with her teacher, Zach. Emily will continue to the next level with him.

This coming month, Emily will attend her first Arthur Murray Showcase held in the Crown Plaza in Foster City. This is an all-day event, starting at 9:00 a.m. and ending at 10:00 p.m. While attendance is not required, many of the serious students and their instructors from Bay Area Arthur Murray classes will be there. All the top teachers will critique the dancers on all levels of skill and style. Emily is looking forward to this event because of the chance to assess her performance and witness others. Mainly, however, she is going just because it is fun.

When I asked Emily what she gets out of her newfound passion that makes dancing so valuable to her, she had several responses. She said she finds joy in the music, in the moment, pleasure in moving in sync with another body, visceral touching and the right hand connection, a firm grip. She added that this new experience has changed her life and has taken her out of her comfort zone. Zach, her teacher, taught her this motto: "Avoid resistance to change." She now lives by that, enjoying this new experience every time she enters the dance floor. So the adventure continues! When I asked her how far she intended to go, she replied, "As long as the joy is there!

# On Becoming an Artist
## Nikki King

In 1983 at age 49, I was in graduate school at San Francisco State University studying to become a Marriage, Family, and Child Counselor. As part of my class work, I attended a music therapy workshop. We participants started by lying around in a circle while the leaders played the music of Debussy. It was very evocative music. After the music ended, the lights were turned up, and we were given a piece of white paper. We saw a pile of colored papers with scissors and glue in the center of our circle. We were told to place anything we felt like on the paper.

During this time, my mother was very ill, so I frequently thought of her and her coming death. But I was not aware of this when I cut and glued all those things on paper. My composition showed a coffin in the foreground with dark clouds above and a shadowy figure rising up and partially covering the moon behind the figure. In my mind, that was my mother's spirit. This was significant, but more importantly, my picture was an excellent composition. I had never in my life had any indication I had that kind of ability.

I continued working on collage at home and eventually started taking collage classes at U. C. Extension in San

Francisco. My teachers were very encouraging and they urged me to make slides of the collages I created in class and submit them to art shows. I struck gold in the first show to which I applied. It was the prestigious Crocker Museum's Northern California Artist Show in Sacramento. Once I got into that show, I thought to myself, "Well, I must be an artist." In the beginning, when I started creating art, I had no idea of the value of my work. I just knew I was satisfied with it. But when I started taking classes and the teachers thought my work was really good, I began to realize that I was an artist. That was twenty-five years ago.

After retirement I continued to broaden my creative horizons by learning jewelry-making, producing brooches and necklaces, as well as learning to paint with pastels.

How intriguing that my career in counseling led to another creative path in art.

# He
Judith Klausner

Bathed in silken fragrances,

Tub rimmed in sweetest fruits,

Pomegranates sucked sweet,

Surrounded by Asher's royal dainties,

I dreamed of tomorrow.


When kissed and circled in gold,

Words floated upward to scorched sky,

Shaded only by the *chuppah* tree.

Wrapped in alcelon lace,

I dreamed of the days of love.

I did not know then,

I would be shattered by the loss.

# I Stand at the Door of Memory
## Leona Biddle

I stand at the door of memory with my eyes closed. It is then I hear the sound of the noon siren in the small town of Aberdeen, Idaho, my first destination after emigrating from Denmark in 1950. This siren transports me immediately back to Odense, Denmark, during WWII. I was just eight when the war started.

That night, I woke with a start, frightened, knowing that this might mean more air raids. Father told me to cover my pajamas quickly and follow the rest of the family to the air raid shelter in the cellar below the six apartments in our building. He was on duty that night as an air raid warden. He would see that all the occupants on all three floors were safely escorted to the cellar.

This was not a new experience for any of us. The sirens blew often, sometimes again and again on the same night. Like mummies in our pajamas covered with coats, we descended without a peep and no lights showing, not even a flashlight to guide us; it was blackouts at all times.

When we reached the cellar, it was already crowded. We found our chairs and huddled together. It was the coldest winter ever, with no heat or fire to warm us. Many had brought blankets. Babies were crying as their mothers cradled and rocked them to sleep. Strange odors and smells emanated from so many different people breathing in and out!

I counted to see if we were all there: the Rasmussens and their two-year-old, the Jensens with the baby, the Madsens and their teen sons, the Jorgensens and their two girls, two and five. I couldn't find the Swan family. I wondered, should I find my father and tell him so he could go look for them? It was with relief I heard rustling and all five Swans appeared in the doorway. Quietly, they found their places.

My older sister Ditte and older brother John were arguing about the seating. I sat by my mother. I leaned closer for some warmth to rub off her.

Everyone was quieting down, as if fearful that if they spoke, an RAF pilot might hear and drop their bombs on our house. Their mission was to follow the lights lit by Danish Underground fighters and bomb the factories that were now turned into war-making facilities. We knew from past experience that sometimes the bombs would fail their mission and the drop would hit our apartment houses or shops.

I clenched my book and flashlight, hoping to get away with reading now. We were in a secure room and no lights would show. I would feel safer if my father was with us. He'd know what to do if a bomb hit nearby. He was standing watch.

It seemed like many hours went by before the all-clear siren sounded, but it was only forty minutes and we were safe. In silence, we all struggled up the stairs to bed once more, hoping we would be lucky and not have another siren go off this night.

# Grand Entrance
Sally Tilbury

Acapulco, the popular Mexican tourist destination, was more appealing in the '60s, but then, everything has a rosier look when you are young and you walk on the beach holding hands. It doesn't matter exactly what year it was. All I remember is I was young and thin and wore a white skirt  with knife-sharp pleats, a navy blazer and pumps, and those blue and white shoes we called "spectators."

The Acapulco Hilton was newly completed. The lobby was dramatic, with high ceilings and tile floors. The manager invited us to see the Presidential Suite on the top floor. We had never seen such luxurious appointments. The spacious rooms were cooled by overhead fans. So Hemingway. Ocean breezes whooshed in through tall open windows. All outdoors twittered with bird chatter. There were potted palms on cool tile floors and hand-woven fabrics of the most intense colors.

The hotel operation did have its glitches. Frequent electrical failures were exasperating. Guests were cross when the lights went out, but we were young and who needs lights. The management worked double-time to make everything run smoothly. There were gardeners, painters, and engineers hurrying to make everything right. Nothing worked, but it looked grand. Newly planted bougainvillea cascaded over garden walls. These grounds would be lush in no time.

We left the Presidential Suite, entered the elevator, and began our descent. The elevator jerked to a stop midway, but in such total darkness, we could not know which floors we were between. Dark is one thing, a dark elevator, quite another. The manager turned to me and asked if I were frightened. "Not at all," I lied. Inwardly, I vowed I must simply do a mind trip on myself to forget claustrophobia, and above all, stay cool. It would be over soon. Poise is a job.

The manager and Chuck forced the doors open, and there, far below us, in daylight, was what appeared to be the kitchen with tile floor. Many men looked up toward the ceiling at the three of us stranded, the floor of the elevator a few feet below the high ceiling. Young men in white jackets must be chefs and busboys, I thought. Responding to the manager's barking orders to get a chair for *Señora*, they placed a chair strategically under our elevator and reached toward me.

Was I scared? You bet. I sat on the floor of the elevator, carefully tucked my skirt in at my sides, then stretched my feet toward the chair. It was the same action as getting down from a high fence. I reached, pointed and jumped, confident I was going to make it. Arms reached up to break my fall. I was caught by helping hands who guided my feet to the chair. It was daylight. Unfortunately, my pleated skirt had gone up over my head, but was quickly smoothed down. I blinked in the light. I heard applause, then laughter.

I had landed in the lobby of the Acapulco Hilton.

# My Smoking Days
Hal Peters

Entertainment in my home town of Dixon, California, population 1,100, was almost totally limited to the movie theater, where pictures changed three times weekly. Sunday and Monday were the "A" films: musicals, dramas, and the ones with established stars in them. Tuesdays through Thursdays were mixed bag days, but Fridays and Saturdays usually displayed a double feature: a B-grade western and a B-grade gangster flick. Everyone smoked in these films, except in the westerns, where the heroes abstained. Legends like Gene Autry, Roy Rogers, William Boyd, *aka* Hopalong Cassidy, never raised a smoke to their lips. They were the "good guys" and role models. However, they were literally the only actors in any movies who didn't smoke on screen.

At age seven, my friends and I would often play "Cowboys," "Cops and Robbers," or war games, and our gear was as authentic as possible. To truly emulate the actors, smoking naturally came into play. Our home was on an acre of land with neighbors on one side of the property. Large shrubs, trees, and hedges were prevalent, thus providing an abundance of hiding places. We had little forts everywhere plus a vacant lot across the street with a row of junipers that provided another off campus hideout. We averaged only one cigarette during a "play day," so supplies lasted a long time, plus not all my buddies indulged.

Cigarettes during World War II were among the luxuries that were extremely difficult to obtain. Other everyday staples like sugar, butter, meat, fish, and candy were unavailable to most civilians, but not to those whose livelihood supported the war effort, like my father's sheep ranches, which provided meat and wool for our troops. My dad stored supplies in a garage at our home, which he took to the hired hands each week. I had access to that garage where cartons of *Wings* cigarettes were kept. *Wings* were extra-long cigarettes and appealing to me and my chums, as each pack contained a card with a drawing of an airplane on it from Allied or Axis countries. They were traded like baseball cards, but on a much smaller scale, because they were so scarce to the civilian population. In Dixon, I practically cornered the market. *Bull Durhams* were yet another smoke available. They came with tobacco paper requiring you to "roll your own" which called for considerable talent, and was time-consuming and often disastrous.

There was a breath sweetener called *Sen-Sen* that wasn't rationed. It consisted of small *Tic-Tac*-sized licorice packed in 2"x 2" paper packs. It was quite popular with smokers wishing to disguise their breaths. We always used it before interacting with our parents! Our clothes weren't that tell-tale because nearly everyone smoked or had the odor of tobacco in their homes.

At about the age of eight or nine, I was walking with my dad along a levee on the Haas Slough at the Duck Club, one of his eight ranches, when he casually inquired, "Your mother tells me you're a smoker, is that right?"

Wow! My heart stopped, I choked a bit and then stammered, "I guess so." I had absolutely no idea that my mom was even remotely suspicious! Next, he offered me one of his *Chesterfields*, the cigarette most recommended by doctors. Then he lit it for me. After that, I had two more, way above my daily norm, and didn't cough or choke as I made a conscious effort to inhale.

Nothing more was ever said about that incident. I wasn't scolded, forced to quit, or asked how I was obtaining the cigarettes so naturally with my trips to the garage. To this day, I've never learned why I wasn't punished or at least forced to have a discussion with my parents. They were having major marital problems then, so this might have seemed trivial.

My closest pal, Glen Wilson, and I were about ten when we won corn cob pipes at the Dixon fair. Initially, we blew bubbles in them, but when I happened upon a tin of Prince Albert pipe tobacco in the garage, we knew where it was supposed to go. Pipe smoking made us feel more mature. Plus, we didn't have to inhale, and it smelled good.

After we finished the initial find, I spotted a can of *Lucky Strike* pipe tobacco in our basement, and Glen and I lit up. Apparently, this was extremely old stuff, because we simultaneously became deathly ill and made it to the front steps of our house, where we sat and watched the world spin around us at jet-like velocity. My mom found us there when she returned that afternoon and suspected that something was disturbing us. We explained we were nauseous because we must have eaten something that didn't agree with us.

That ended my smoking at age ten. Sports took over in our lives instead of cowboys and Indians.

# A Hard Lesson Learned
## Nancy Humphriss

Summer had arrived, school was out, and my best friend Mary and I were on our way to the public library, our book bags filled with books to return. This would be a weekly affair, and one we enjoyed on many levels. We were both avid readers, and at age eleven, we had many secrets to share, as well as gossip to exchange.

Easthampton, Massachusetts, was a small town, population approximately 10,000, with close families, neighbors, and friends, all-knowing and watching out for each other. Our walk from the outskirts of town was about two miles, first along a wide road with scattered houses along the way before reaching the more populated areas. As we walked and chatted, we would occasionally stop at a home where the owners had a small fudge-making business. If there were any broken chocolate scraps, the owners would give us a small bag of delicious pieces of fudge to enjoy. Then we descended down a short hill, and crossed a bridge over the Manhan River, more a large brook than a river, where we would stop and watch the ducks paddling around or occasional swimmers cooling off. Farther on, we passed the house where Mary's grandmother lived, and if she happened to be out sitting in her rocker on her porch, we would stop there and chat as well. This, too, frequently meant a cookie or two along with a glass of milk.

We were now on the main road entering the town. As we started to climb the hill on the last leg of our journey, a car stopped, and a man opened his side window and called to us. We stopped and waited to hear what he had to say. "Could you help me, young ladies? I'm new here and I'm looking for the library. I have books to sell, but I can't seem to find my way there."

Our response was spontaneous and enthusiastic. "Oh, yes, we know how to find the library. As a matter of fact, we're on our way there now! We could show you!"

"Great!" he responded. "Hop in and I'll take you there." Delighted to have a ride up the hill and to our destination, we eagerly joined him, Mary and I both in the back seat. We traveled slowly, stopping at a few red lights, but proceeding to our destination. Just before we reached the library, we suddenly heard police sirens and saw red lights flashing behind us. Our friend pulled over and stopped, and two policemen approached the car, guns drawn.

"Get out! Put your hands on the top of the car, and spread your legs!" they shouted. Mary and I were aghast and afraid. What had we done? What had our friend done?

The man protested loudly, and in agitated tones he asked, "Why are you doing this? I have done nothing wrong! I'm a book salesman and these young ladies were nice enough to offer to show me the way to the library. I have an appointment with Mrs. Phillips, the head librarian, to sell her some books!"

The two policemen then made us get out of the car and sit in the police cruiser. "We'll just check out your excuse, so one of us will go with you to the library, and my partner will follow with the girls."

As it turned out, our rather naïve book salesman was just that, rushing to a scheduled meeting with Mrs. Phillips. She was perplexed and upset by the incident, and after checking everyone out, the police let him go with admonitions about picking up girls willy-nilly. It seems someone who knew us had seen us getting in a stranger's car and alerted the police.

Now it was our turn to be admonished by the police and Mrs. Phillips. By now I heard in my head my parents' constant admonition: "Never, never accept a ride with a stranger!"

How many times had I heard that? Mary, too, had the same message given to her. Now waves of what lay ahead at home overcame me, and I started to cry. "Please, please don't tell my mother!" I begged. "I have learned my lesson, a lesson I'll never forget! I promise I'll never do anything like this again!"

The police and Mrs. Phillips consulted each other, and at last decided to trust us and not tell our parents. Vastly relieved, we then did our library thing and finally hurried home, vowing never to tell anyone about what happened that day.

A few days later, I found my parents standing in the living room, looking extremely upset and angry. "What now?" I asked myself. It seems the local paper had a column called "Police Activity," and Mary and I found ourselves in the headlines. There was no way out now, and the punishment followed. Of course a hearty and angry lecture occurred, with all the expected "How could you be so easily conned?" and "How many times did we tell you . . ." statements. Then no allowance for a month. And even worse, no radio time, which meant I'd miss my favorite programs, "Abbot and Costello," "I Love a Mystery," and the best, "The Shadow." A whole month! But one thing not taken away was my reading time. I still had Nancy Drew to keep me occupied.

# A CHRISTMAS MEMORY
### Karin Fitzgerald

We sat by the fire that cold winter night,
Watching the snow turn everything white.

Our thoughts were of Christmas, the very next day,
Dinner at our house, that's always the way.

There'd be clove-studded ham with salads and fruit,
And plenty of wine, we all liked the Brut.

We talked about family, it made both of us smile,
We'd all be together in a very short while.

The fir tree smelled fresh and glistened with treasure,
Some old and some new, too many to measure.

The gifts were all placed and circled the tree,
Each present had meaning and filled me with glee.

The traditions we kept, some sweet and some funny,
But one was a favorite and really a honey.

The dill pickle ornament was the necessary given,
In the tree's dark green branches it was already hidden.

This was the rule when the children all had arrived,
They'd gather round the tree like bees in a hive.

On tiptoe they'd stretch or squat down so low,
Looking and hoping to spy the green glow.

Finding the pickle is a very big deal,
The first child to find it always lets out a squeal.

The reward was the opening of the very first gift,
The losers might grumble, but their laughter was swift.

Full of joy for tomorrow, we jumped into bed,
And thought we heard Santa getting out of his sled.

# Mother Knows Best
## Leona Biddle

Mother asks, "Where are you going?"

"Don't you remember? It's Saturday. Jytte and I are going to the movies."

"Wish I had time to see a movie," Mother replies.

"You wouldn't like it."

"What are you going to see?"

"Oh, Mother, Mother, please! We're in a hurry! We'll miss the beginning!"

"*Ja, ja*, but you have time to be civil."

"It's the *Romance Down on the Farm* series playing at the Kino. Oh, please, please! I'll tell you all about it after!"

"Did you change your underwear? It's just off the line, maybe slightly damp." Mother can't help herself; she talking about the other one of two I own.

My head is out the door. "*Ja, ja. . .*"

"Did you hear me? It's newer, with a strong elastic top!"

I turn to my friend and whisper, "Jytte, I'm sorry; you know how mothers are."

Jytte and I fly down the stairs and out into the summer air.

"You didn't change, did you?" Jytte says.

"No, we wouldn't make the bus, and we'd miss the beginning. I just pray that my old pair will hold up. Mother was right; they are a bit loose."

We hurry along. "Aren't you sick of wartime rationing, Jytte? Did you know my older sister Ditte feeds string through the top of her panties and ties it in a bow? *Ha ha ha.* You can tell when she wears them by the little bulge it makes. What about you?"

"My Mom squirreled stuff like elastic away in her sewing box, so we're OK."

Focused on making the bus, arm in arm, we skip along Nyborgsvej's sidewalk at a fast pace.

"Look, Mette," Jytte says, pointing. "Clydesdale horses pulling the beer wagon."

"When will we ever get petrol again?"

Then, as we rush past the laundry, "*Uhmm!* Smell the fresh, laundered sheets. It's like perfume in the air. I can even hear the swish of the ironing machines."

Jytte looks at the handsome postman whizzing by on his yellow bicycle. "I just love his red jacket with gold braid and buttons, and how his hat matches. And look at all that mail in his black bag. I wonder who it's for. Wish it was for me. I'm going to marry a postman some day!"

"How do you know that?"

"I just love everything about getting mail."

"Jytte, we made it!" We're finally at the post marked yellow for a bus stop. We take some deep breaths.

"What a long line," Jytte says. "But look! There's our yellow bus, just coming over the top of the hill."

With a laugh I say, "It's just sheer joy being here, going to the movies, free from cares." But silently, I pray to God, "Please, please let my panties stay up!"

The bus finally inches its way into the bus slot. A few riders get off, and at last, it's my turn, right behind Jytte. With my foot on the first step and a hand on the rail, I stop, startled to feel a slither and a tickle over my hips and on down. I tell myself, "You can't look down! Now what?" A light comes on.

I smile, lift my head, and smartly step out of the panty puddle at my feet. I enter the bus, and with relief, sink down next to Jytte.

No one asks, "Who left their panties on the ground?"

I laugh and Jytte joins me. She doesn't even know why. I laugh until I cry and folks turn in their seats to smile at such happy girls.

Finally, Jytte gasps, "What happened?"

I manage to choke out, "My. . . my panties! I feel so free. . ."

More laughter all the way to the movie.

Yes, Mother knows best.

# The Curtain Opened
Sally Tilbury

Beware of fourteen-year-old girls. They are full of imaginative schemes. On a Sunday morning in 1967, our daughter, Peggy, knelt on the living room floor and read the want ad section of the *Los Angeles Sunday Times.* Suddenly, she looked up and asked, "Mom, what is a 'supernumerary'? And what is an 'assistant to a supernumerary'?"

"Why do you ask?" I answered from my position at the sink. I dried my hands and stumbled around with an answer for her. I explained it was a term for a type of extra, or an assistant to the star, or part of the supporting cast, a walk-on. In any case, it would be a background part. These parts were often given to young aspiring students or members of the troupe, and sometimes they might carry the wood across the stage, or a potted palm. They are sometimes an assistant to the star. Perhaps they might hold the star's skirt. I suggested she look it up.

She had been reading the ads and I had a premonition she was scheming to try out as an extra in the New York City Opera's production of Handel's *Julius Caesar*, which was coming to the new Los Angeles Music Center. A mother must use all her powers of premonition to think ahead of fourteen-year-old girls. Some children wake up each morning and say, "Guess what?" Beware.

Peg phoned her friend, Cathy, who arrived on the double, and together they schemed even further. The girls began to use all their persuasive talents on me—hadn't I always wanted to see the backstage costume and makeup rooms at the new Music Center? And the Green Room? Besides, they had nothing to do, a common lament among teenagers. They were suffering unbearable boredom. It would be a perfect excursion for this long afternoon, they said, and they assured me they did not expect to qualify, but just watch. I began to have my doubts about this plot.

I called Cathy's mother and asked her permission, and the girls and I were away on the nineteen-mile drive to the Music Center. We stood in a long line waiting to be called before the Italian Director. We heard one of the two young men ahead of us say to the other, "I memorized the first act, how about you?" The girls looked at me with panic and dismay. I was busy peeking into the costume rooms and shrugged to remind them this was their idea and there was no escaping now. They had signed in.

The door opened and about sixty people flocked in. Peggy would later describe them as all "big people." The Italian Director looked at Peggy and Cathy as they entered the room. Extending his arm, he pointed toward them with two fingers, signaling to his assistant that he wanted to interview those two and would they step forward. The girls were a matching pair.

Now I panicked. From the rear of the room I wondered what we were getting into. What would Cathy's parents say? What next? I moved to the front of the room to listen to the girls being questioned. Would they be able to get released from school for practices?

"Of course."

Had they been in prior productions?

"Of course." They continued to stretch the truth with great aplomb. I thought of the fun the girls had in the junior high production of *The Music Man*, but this opera was to be the real thing.

Were they serious students of the Ballet?

"Of course." I could not help but think of the two dollars we left on the piano at the nearby neighborhood dance studio for Peggy.

The opera was to be done in 17$^{th}$ Century High Baroque. They would be ladies-in-waiting to the star. They would wear hoop skirts together with tall turbans. There would be fittings. I was asked to come forward and give my approval and assure the manager the girls had their Social Security numbers.

"Our first professional performance!" they said over and over as they jumped up and down in the back of the car like six-year-olds. I had my doubts. What had I done?

We returned to Cathy's house where I would confess the girls had succeeded in being officially hired. Surprise! Cathy's mother was delighted. She said the girls were so talented and would it not be a grand experience and should we not break out a bottle of champagne to celebrate? I was sunk. This, after all, was going to be a real opera at the grandest theatre in Los Angeles and I was a conspirator. Should we continue this misadventure?

The following week I appeared at the office of Paul Revere Junior High to ask for their early release on the days of practice. The office was pleased to give us permission. This was too easy. Cathy's mother drove the first carpool. On the day of dress rehearsal, I accompanied the girls backstage. On the way to the costume department, we spotted Norman Treagle being outfitted with a padded muscle suit in his dressing room. Treating them like old pros, the no-nonsense makeup lady stood in front of her battery of makeups and brushes and asked them, "Are you light Egyptian or medium?"

Again they were as cool as though they knew what she was talking about. "Medium," they shrugged. They were transformed with huge black eyes like cats by the makeup department. The dressers then dropped the extremely large hoop skirts over the girls' heads, followed by the tall turbans. I hardly recognized them.

The night of the first performance arrived. Backstage, each of the girls was given a sawhorse to perch on, since their hoop skirts prevented them from using a chair. When it was their cue, Peg hopped off the sawhorse and knocked it down with a resounding clang. She still remembers the scorn of all the stagehands. The Italian Director was frantic.

When the curtain slowly opened, we four parents held our breaths. There, in perfect and elegant *port de bras* position, one hand over the heart, the other extended, the two girls, looking poised and aloof, proceeded slowly and gracefully down the staircase on either side of Beverly Sills.

# A Message and a Dream
## Shirley Johnson

When I awoke one morning years ago and remembered having dreamed about Ingrid Ostberg, I was surprised and puzzled. How did she, of all the people that I knew from my small home town in northern Minnesota, appear in my sleep? I had never known her well. She was two years ahead of me at school, a tall, pleasant, quiet student who went home directly after classes and didn't seem to spend time with anyone that I knew. She lived on the outskirts of town and could choose to take the bus home or to walk, if she preferred. I rarely saw her in town.

The truth is, I only remember her when she came to the movies with her mother. I sold tickets at my father's theater and remember her paying for one adult and one child. I don't think that in those days we used the term "teenager," but even then, most high school students wouldn't have wanted to be seen with a parent at the movies. Her mother looked pleasant, but old-fashioned compared to other mothers, and her father, Halvor Ostborg, a Swedish immigrant, was rather a mystery. I had heard that he was very strict and perhaps abusive, but I knew nothing for certain.

However, when she put down her thirty-five cents, I felt sorry for her and imagined that she must be lonely, a somewhat withdrawn outsider in the small group of young people in our town.

I don't believe I thought about Ingrid until some thirty years later when I took my mother to the movies. She had moved to live with me in California, and when I put down five dollars for our tickets, I remembered the quiet girl I had slightly known in High School.

A day or so after my dream in which she appeared, I received a letter from her. I was not only surprised but somewhat shaken by the coincidence. She told me that she was living in a small town in South Dakota with her husband, a Lutheran minister, and two children. Getting her letter astonished me. How did she know where I lived or what my married name was? It must have taken some trouble for her to find me in those days before Facebook or Google.

I choose to call it an amazing coincidence, although I am not entirely at ease with that answer. I am by nature a realist and do not feel comfortable in calling it mental telepathy, but to have heard from Ingrid after thirty some years immediately following a dream in which she suddenly appeared, does seem too unlikely to be simply chance.

However I explain it, I was touched by her message. She told me that she had been thinking of me and was moved to write to say how much she had appreciated my cheerfulness when she came to the theater with her mother, and in general to thank me for my kindness to her when we were young.

I wrote to thank her, of course, and we did not correspond further. I don't remember whether I told her about my dream. Probably not. In my many moves since then, I have lost her address, but I always think of her when talk of unlikely coincidences comes up.

# My Zadye's Alcove
Judith Klausner

Usually, during the week, my mother took my older brother and me from the North Shore of Chicago to the Loop for an afternoon at Goodman Children's Theater, a brace tightening at the dentists', or perhaps an afternoon at the Art Institute or the Field Museum. Many of these days we stopped off to see my grandfather, Zadye Levin. Zadye had a tailor shop tucked away under the elevated trains on East Van Buren Street in the heart of the Loop. For me, his tailor shop was a world of atmosphere, discovery, and human warmth that I could not actually describe at my young age. But when I think back now, what I felt was a *hamish* (family) love. The fondness not only came from my Zadye but also from the pressers and the odd group of men seated in booths waiting for their pants to be pressed. They read *The Daily Forward,* a Yiddish newspaper. As I skipped by them, they would smile or say in Yiddish, "*Mein kindalah,*" and ruffle my blond corkscrew curls.

A sign hung askew, grime-ridden and fading in the front windows: *PANTS PRESSED WHILE YOU WAIT.* That was Zadye's only advertisement.

The doors were always open to let out the steam from

the pressing machines and the flies flew inside the shop, usually dying on the windowsills, where they piled up until a slight breeze might blow away the first layer. The little bit of air from the open door helped lessen the smell of the sweat from the four pressers as the perspiration rolled down their bodies. The pressers were centered in the middle of the room. The men who worked the large machines appeared to be fat, perspiring and tired. But they would stop for a second as I ran around them to pat my head with their sweaty hands.

I peeked out of the open door several times to see if the horses were coming. For some unknown reason, I was rarely disappointed. Two Chicago policemen arrived right at the door of the store on magnificent horses as they rode through the Loop. When I ran outside to the sidewalk, the handsome and dignified policemen reached into their pockets and gave me a small piece of wrapped-up apple and carefully instructed me how to feed the treat to their horses. I think now these stalwart riders must have had many treats they gave to many children along their route. What a magical time it was!

The most wonderful thing about Zadye's shop was hidden in an alcove in the back, out of sight. The alcove contained a large black safe. The dial of the safe was always set so it would open immediately with a slight jiggle of the handle. The treasures of the world were contained inside. I would look up at my Zadye with imploring eyes and he would say, "You may look, my *kindalah.*" There were large dusty boxes of buttons of every color and shape. There were penknives, large and small, and I knew I was not allowed to try and open the little blades. It was full of wondrous things that the men on the seats accidently left when they put on their newly pressed pants. Zadye would always put the forgotten items in the safe. Rarely did anyone return for them. I found scraps of paper filled with notes, and even snapshots of a family or loved one.

I was always hoping Zadye would see me caressing a jeweled pin or ring. I knew, of course, that whatever I held the longest in my hand would be given to me. I never asked, and I never left without some treasure. I once found a purple ring. It was the color I loved. It became mine. When I was a teenager many years later, my mother took the ring to a jeweler. She had a hint that it might be real. The amazing amethyst stone was placed beautifully in white gold filigree, magnificent and very old. The amethyst had not lost its color and it was mine. I wore that ring with pride and joy and love until I was well into my sixties, when I moved from my home to another one after my husband died. It was lost and I never saw it again. I still mourn its loss. Perhaps I mourn for the man who lovingly gave it to me and the memories of those decades long past.

In the alcove, Zadye amassed whatever possessions he had. The alcove was his business office, the place to help others with problems, and his spot to make small real estate deals. Sitting beside this old battered safe with the manufacturer's label worn away with age, my Zadye managed to make enough money to have a home on Floronoy Street.

His daughters had fur coats, and his car, my mother told me with pride, had a running board. He was also able to send three children through college. My mother and aunt both became teachers. His son, Meyer Levin, graduated from the University of Chicago at the age of eighteen and became one of the great writers of our time.

It was from his alcove that he led a fine life. My Bubbe and Zadye both read and spoke English without an accent. Although he was a first generation immigrant, he wanted the best for my Bubbe and his children. He craved for them to be educated. I know now how hard he worked and why.

It was there, both in his alcove and home, that I saw and listened to his friends: the Yonkels, Hymies and Abes. They read, in English, the works of Malamud and Charyn and Singer. In his store front I danced and sang while the Simons and Bennies watched him watch me. My Zadye didn't understand me, nor did his customers and friends. They didn't even try. But they still patted my head, a special Jewish pat, with love in their eyes and hands. It was a touch to say, "We love you just because you are ours to love."

It is the intense love of my Zadye and Bubbe and the other grandparents of that generation that is a memorial to their world...and ours. It was the giving without question I was fortunate to receive and remember. It is this tenderness writers like Bernard Malamud, Saul Bellow, Neil Simon, Jakob Wassermann, Meyer Levin, and so many more wrote about and memorialized.

But are these memories enough to cause that close nostalgic feeling I still have for my Jewish heritage? Is it enough to say, "The best thing that ever happened to me was that I was born a Jew? I, who cannot read Hebrew prayers except those I memorized. Can I even wonder how it came to be that I married a prominent rabbi and became a real *Rebbetzin*? Was it no wonder that my children are all educated and living loving lives with their own families who follow our ways. I feel it is a blessing.

Looking back, I know my Zayde at seventy was not the same as our seventy. He looked different. He had a slower step, a sadness in his eyes, creases in his skin. And his voice was softer. He received less attention. He gave more love, but it was not heard or felt as much as before. It was inside of him where we could hardly see or hear it. It was locked away like the treasures he gave to me. It is the tenderness of our modern Sholen Aleichems, long may they write. Perhaps there is hope for a feeling of warmth and love in our future.

As the revered Eli Wiesel wrote, "I write so the future generations will have a viable tradition to pass on to my children." So it was, and so it is.

# Surprise
### Floyd Schlosser

"I formerly wanted to be perfect, and then discovered that place had already been taken."

# Her List
## Jack Russ

Before I retired, my wife did all the family grocery shopping. She was quite adept at finding new foods and talented at preparing many delightful and imaginative meals. We had often entertained neighbors, business acquaintances, and family. Once the kids left, her activities expanded. The pressure grew to reciprocate the hospitality these new friends had extended to us. This growing level of activity led to her "suggestion" that I take on some of the simpler chores she had done previously to provide more time for her new undertakings. Sounded good to her. I'm sure. I had other ideas.

It took me less than a week to learn to do the laundry. She was fussy about my mixing colored garments in the same wash with white pieces. I smiled and did the task the way she wanted—most of the time. However, I did convince her I was too clumsy to iron clothing, especially any of her stuff.

Over time, a pattern of routine tasks began to take shape. I got in a round of golf every week or two. Routine car care wasn't an issue. Stepping back into yard work went okay after I'd updated my garage tool collection. My son came by several times to refresh me on some of the details of frequent minor household repairs. I'd been able, so far, to work at my own pace; well, most of the time. But, my wife's greater "free" time worked like a magnet to collect a plague of little jobs for me.

Yesterday morning she said, "I need some things at the market," as she headed toward the door with an armload of packages. She paused, set her packages on the table, and searched through the stuff in her purse. She pulled out a wrinkled yellow notepad page and handed it to me. Another search of her purse came up with four little slips of paper that looked as though they had been torn from the newspaper. Discount coupons, I figured.

"You have the time today," she said, "and I don't. Donna is waiting for me out in front. Besides, you don't have anything important to do." Before closing the door, she paused and said, "I expect to be back by 4:00. I may need some help fixing a special dish for tonight."

Her list was reasonably short, but missing specifics, like a brand name, for instance, and how much or how many of some items.

Mid-afternoon, when I drove up to Cooper's Market, there was a parking spot open right in front. A good indicator for the challenge ahead, I thought. I selected one of the shopping carts from the several aligned before the entry, went in, looked around, and paused. I'd better have a plan.

First, the shopping list. Where was it? Not in my pocket. Did I leave it at home? No. I had it in the car. Sure enough, it was on the passenger seat when I went back. Those discount chits were paper clipped to the shopping list. So, back in the market. Now, where to begin?

Cooper's Market was new. I'd followed my wife there only once before, but didn't remember where things were. This time I'd just wander around and find the things on the list. There weren't many.

I passed through the section with the milk and cheese. She didn't have milk on the list, but I could use a fresh carton. There wasn't enough left in the refrigerator for my breakfast cereal in the morning. I got two.

Cheese was next on the list. I found the display on the next aisle. Which cheese was I supposed to get? Her list didn't say. The cheese display section must have had a hundred varieties and packages. The only cheese name I could recall from one of her more recent comments was Monterey Jack. After a longer-than-expected search, I found some larger packages of solid pieces. Her list didn't say how much to buy. Two Monterey Jacks went into my cart to cover the unexpected. It seemed to me that should be enough, although I had no idea how she planned to use it. Farther along the display, I found a package of shredded Monterey Jack cheese and next to it a special package of the Jack cheese with another unfamiliar name. The name seemed to be Italian, but the package was displayed as new and special. I put the two large cheeses, a package of shredded, and one of the special offerings in my cart.

Eggs were next on her list. They were displayed across the aisle from the cheese collection. I had always thought of an egg as, well, as an egg. Not so here. There were three different sizes displayed. They all looked the same to me, except the group with brown shells. I wondered what made them different. Other than shell color, they were the same as the white-shelled kind. Why not experiment? A single carton of the brown ones joined a carton of the large white eggs in my cart, in case she had a preference.

Coffee was next. I found the brand we'd been using, but was surprised to see how many different types and brands were displayed. An easy decision there. One of the familiar packages went into my cart. No, considering how much coffee we consumed, I loaded two packages.

In the fruit and vegetable section, I rescued a bunch of bananas and six oranges. Her list didn't include oranges. How many should I get? They would give me a pleasant addition to my lunch. We also were out of berries for my breakfast cereal, so I selected two clear plastic packages of raspberries. What was next on the list?

As I passed the bakery section, they were displaying a shelf of warm, freshly baked, sugar-coated breakfast rolls. That was too good to pass up. I packaged four for my next breakfast and took a fifth to eat in the car on the way back to the house.

Next on the list was sliced meat—but again, she hadn't noted which meat or how much. I could hear her angry chatter when I came home with the wrong variety. And, how much? Why hadn't she told me? This was taking longer than I had planned, so, *Be decisive*, my brain urged. I loaded a package of sliced turkey breast, one of sliced bacon and one of baloney for sandwiches. I didn't select any fish. She had strong feelings about fish in general. I chose to avoid a hassle by skipping fish. However, a nearby package of chicken pieces looked appetizing, so I added a large one. The cart was filling fast.

The last item on the list was illegible, so I skipped it.

The checkout lines were busier than expected, but after about ten minutes, I'd moved up to one customer short of the checkout clerk. I dug out my wallet, preparing to slide my credit card when it was my turn.

No card. I had it yesterday. Now what?

The clerk asked me to slide a Cooper's Market card through the card reader to take advantage of their special discounts. I didn't have one. Never had one. Now what?

The people in line behind me were becoming agitated at my delay.

I explained to the clerk all I had was cash and that was $1.20 less than the bill.

We negotiated.

I gave back the package of chicken and paid cash for the balance and completely forgot the discount coupons clipped to the shopping list.

My wife had said to expect her return about 4:00. I scrambled to unload the groceries and store them in the kitchen in their usual locations. I put the last raspberry package in the refrigerator as my wife came in the door. Before I could begin to relate my carefully rehearsed explanation for my buying spree, she said, "I met Marilyn this afternoon. We are joining them for dinner at her house about 5:30 for cocktails and one of her special Italian dishes. I didn't feel like cooking tonight, anyway."

# Game On: Hurray for Hockey
Karin Fitzgerald

I pull the collar of my husband's beautiful old raccoon coat firmly around my ears. He can't be at the game today, but he's loaned me his coat, which is almost a presence in itself. He paid an old Alaskan who was heading to warmer climes $50 for this treasure and it's in great condition. The coat hangs down over my fleece-lined boots and is so heavy it barely moves as I stamp my feet on the packed-down snow.

I look at the other parents who are bundled up in parkas and furs. We're standing in a row along the outside of the "boards." This four-foot-high solid wood fence separates the onlookers from players, and it encloses and defines the outer perimeter of the big sheet of ice on this outdoor rink. All of us are here because our sons are going to play a hockey game today. Each team represents different areas of our small city and all of the teams are sponsored by the Anchorage Hockey Association.

We cheer and clap as the boys skate onto the ice. The two teams merge and begin their warm-up drill. They skate down the length of the ice, circle around the end, and back up the other side; around and around they skate in a big, easy flowing "river" of hockey players. We know that rocky shoals and unseen currents await these young warriors in the contest that lies ahead. More clapping and cheers when the two goalies appear. They slowly skate toward their goalie cages at each end of the rink. They resemble roly-poly Michelin Men in their padded protective gear, but are oddly graceful as they stretch and do amazing splits in front of each netted cage.

We parents smile and talk to each other. Our breath billows out in gauzy clouds of steam. Most of our cars in the parking lot behind us are turned on for brief periods of time because it's only six degrees above zero today. We're all thankful that the Anchorage pediatricians finally got together and delivered an edict, "No child will be allowed to play hockey outdoors if the temperature drops to ten degrees below zero." Before this, each coach set his own rule about the degree of cold before play would be cancelled and no one was happy.

Most of the boys, like our son, Dennis, have been playing hockey for several years, and even though they're only thirteen or fourteen, they have impressive skill sets. When the referee skates onto the ice, the chatter fades away. Players from each team open a gate in the four-foot wooden fence and sit on benches inside their own "Box." The five kids from each team (one center, two wings and two defensemen) who will begin this first 20-minute period of play take their positions at center ice. A strange quiet descends and we parents all strain forward as if our desire to win is aimed at the two centers who will start the contest. They stand on each side of the ref, bent down, facing each other with their sticks gripped tight and firm on the ice. The ref drops the puck and the game begins as the two centers struggle to capture the puck and pass it to their teammates. We parents straighten up and start to breathe again.

I look at the eager young faces and think about the reasons I love hockey so much. There's the distinctive sound the puck makes when it hits the boards, that resounding *THWACK* is music to my ears. Then there are the times I want to take a picture of remarkable skating, when the tiny shower of ice crystals is thrown up from the skates of a boy who has made a stunning stop or impossible turn. The way I see it, part of hockey is just an icy ballet. You understand this when you see the fluid, seamless way the players flow onto and off the ice during a game; the choreography always changing and always dynamic.

Oh, boy! My full attention returns; the game is really heating up. I watch as a boy on our team breaks away from the pack and stick-handles like a pro. The frozen three-inch-wide black rubber circle looks like it's glued to the end of his stick. He gleefully herds it down the ice and slaps the puck past the goalie into the netted cage. It's a GOAL, and someone yells, "Now *that's* hockey!"

I'm suddenly jolted out of my feeling that all's right with the world when the raucous voice of Mrs. Knowland slices through the air. She's standing several feet away from me and yells some pretty unpleasant things. Her two sons play for the other team and she's very upset that one of our boys scored a goal. Mrs. Knowland is notorious for urging her sons to commit mayhem on the ice. These kids don't have a chance because they're being encouraged by their mother to play "chippy" hockey. Some of us feel sorry for her boys, but we all want her to shut up.

The coaches all take turns officiating at these contests, and today, the referee is our beloved coach, Dempsey Anderson. Dempsey picks up the puck and skates over to Mrs. Knowland, who still gushes out unprintable words. Anxious to hear what's being said, the only sound from the parents is heavy breathing. In a firm, respectful voice he says, "Mrs. Knowland, this game will not continue until you go to your car and stay there."

Shock and disbelief play across her face. She blusters a bit more and glares at Dempsey, but finally understands that she's been handed an irreversible verdict and marches to her car with angry steps. The clapping starts quietly at first, then a crescendo erupts. We are all clapping and almost giddy with relief because Mrs. Knowland has finally met her match. Their mother's denouement makes a huge impression on her two sons and their behavior on the ice improves dramatically.

I don't know it today, but the next year will an exciting one for our son. He will be skating on the newly created All Star team. For the first time, a kid hockey team will make a trip out of Alaska to compete. Their schedule will take them to Seattle, Washington, Van Nuys, California, and White Horse, Canada. Their reputation for clean play, good sportsmanship, and courtesy will precede them. They'll return home as conquering heroes, not because they've won every game, which they won't, but because they are recognized for setting the Gold Standard in Alaska youth hockey with their conduct on and off the ice.

I will continue to wear many hats as I juggle the sports lives of our four young athletes. I relish the titles I've earned: Hockey Mom, Ski Mom, and Horse Mom, but watching hockey is the only time I get to snuggle in that wonderful old raccoon coat.

# A New Generation of Unexpected Consequences
## Elisabeth Levy

Having four grandchildren, not blood-related, but bonded by love, is in itself an unexpected consequence for me. Here are a few snippets of the surprises they've given me:

### Rebecca Levy

Our granddaughter, Rebecca, was about four years old when she spent the weekend with us. Her parents, who lived fifteen minutes away, were out of town. My husband and I, known as Opa and Oma, decided to take her for a walk. It was a beautiful Sunday morning with a blue sky and a few clouds. We had parked near the creek in Greenbrae and gotten out of the car when Rebecca said in demanding voice, "I want my bike! I want to go home and get it! I don't walk!"

"This is really too bad, Rebecca," Opa said. "Your parents are not home, but if you don't want to walk with us, you can stay in the car and wait for us." Grudgingly, she decided she might as well join us. The pathway along the creek was only partially shaded and it started to get hot.

Oma, feeling bad for poor Rebecca, had an idea. "Why don't we walk fast in the sun and slow in the shade?" Unexpectedly, the walk turned out to be great fun. Today Rebecca still loves to walk and is a great athlete.

## David William Rhoads

At the age of eleven, grandson David W. had a sudden growth spurt. Soon he was nearly one head taller than his classmates. That should be fun, but for David W., it was not. He started to hunch over, trying to make himself invisible, and it became a real problem. His concerned mother called me. "What are we going to do?" We decided it would help his ego to let him fly by himself to San Francisco to visit us. A pair of anxious parents sent him off from Las Vegas and a pair of happy grandparents picked him up in San Francisco.

Around our pool we had the most gorgeous agapanthus. I took David W. with me, and as we stood in front of those flowers, almost taller than we were, I said, "Look how beautiful these Lilies of the Nile are! They are proud and so happy to be so tall that they hold their heads high and look around."

The unexpected happened. David W. straightened up, became a scout leader and to this day still walks with his head up.

## Matthew Levy

Before Matthew's family moved to New York, Wednesday was Oma day. In the morning, like clockwork, Rebecca was dropped off by her mother and stayed for the day. Then the rest of her family came, shared dinner, and went home. This happy routine lasted until Rebecca was five years old and Matthew was born.

When the time came and Rebecca had to go to school, Matthew and I enjoyed our time together. We walked to the pool, around our little hill, and up the path, where one day we discovered the deer behind the steep wall. We could not let the deer come over the wall and eat our gorgeous agapanthus! We had to come up with a strategic plan.

We quietly walked close to the wall, peeked over it, and when we saw the deer, we started to bark, loud and hard. The deer always looked at us. If we continued barking, to Matthew's delight, they started to move away. Sometimes they ran, sometimes they walked slowly. It became a weekly game and the agapanthus was safe.

Our home always gave Matthew a special peaceful feeling, so much so that on a visit a couple of years after his family moved to New York, Matthew attempted to stay by hiding in the house, almost causing his family to miss their flight home.

## Alexa Rhoads

Alexa was always the quietest of the four grandchildren. One time her mother and I had an adult conversation and didn't think anything of Alexa standing next to us listening. She surprised us with a very intelligent comment, and I asked her, "How did you know?" Her answer was, "I never miss a beat," and so it still is.

At Christmas/Chanukah time, the Levys came from New York, and the Rhoads traveled from Las Vegas to spend the holidays with us in Marin County. One evening, my husband and I decided to send the parents out for dinner, cook just for the grandkids, and enjoy them by ourselves. Ann informed me that Alexa didn't like peas or any other vegetables; pasta was her favorite dish. We had pasta, chicken, and peas. I asked Alexa if she would like some peas. "A couple," she said. To me, a couple means two, so she got two. A surprised face looked at me and she said, "O.K., a few more." Today she eats pasta with caution and loves vegetables.

# A Life-changing Decision
### Leona Biddle

The large, important-looking yellow envelope was lying on the floor, making it difficult to open the door to our apartment. All our mail was delivered daily through a slot in the door by a red-coated postman with gold stripes on his sleeve and collar who rode a red and yellow bicycle.

It was 1950. I had just turned seventeen and still lived with my parents in an apartment on Osterled 21, Odense, Denmark. It was rare for me to receive mail of any kind, except for an occasional letter from my pen pal in Washington, D.C., and a couple living in Aberdeen, Idaho. I wanted to rip it open. Instead, I inspected the return address. Who could this be from? I read with wonder: "United States Immigration Office, Copenhagen." Finally, I couldn't stand it any longer and carefully cut it open. To my surprise, after two years of waiting, the letter informing me that my immigration visa was approved had arrived!

I was at the crossroads. I had a huge decision to make: to immigrate to the United States or stay in Denmark. This was for real! The decision could only be mine, mine alone!

Was I ready to leave my home, family, friends, and country for the unknown on the other side of the globe? Was I ready to take the leap alone? My close girlfriend, Jytte, and I had planned to do this together. But she had fallen deeply in love and would marry her sweetheart, Mogens, in another year. (They lived happily ever after!)

I pondered my options. There weren't that many, really. If I stayed, I would marry a nice boy. However, it was hard to move upward in the job market. I would forever remain in the workforce, maybe never own a house, a rather bleak future compared to the visions that drew me to the U.S.A., touted as the "Land of Opportunity."

By the time my father, a carpenter, and my mother, a chef at a large hotel restaurant, returned from work, I had made up my mind. It was a big yes! I was ready to go!

But my problems weren't over. I had worked long hours after graduating from high school to earn enough money for my passage, with some additional income from babysitting nights. But I needed more to live on once I arrived in the United States. My family earned just enough to get by and had nothing extra to give me. (As it turned out, one uncle, a wealthy land and cattle owner, rescued me, giving me the $50 allowed at that time to bring into the U.S.A.)

Studying the letter more closely, I learned that it contained numerous forms asking for current health status; doctor's clearance, personal history, former addresses, job information, passport forms, name and address of my sponsor in the U.S.A., and much, much more. There was one document that worried me. My eighteenth birthday fell after my departure date, so who would sign off and approve of my leaving? My parents, my legal guardians, had never expressed their approval or assent!

When I asked, my dad declared he would not sign the petition. His excuse: "If I do, you will always think I wanted to rid myself of my daughter!" My mother, on the other hand, ended up signing for the opposite reason. I was a strong-willed daughter and she knew that. She told me, "You will never forgive me if I stop you from following your heart."

# Clutter
Dorothy Herbert

Clutter surrounds me. It piles up on all available flat surfaces.

It mocks my natural instinct for order and frustrates my attempts at organizing.

And yet it keeps me company and at times comforts me.

I am not alone. The world has not forgotten me.

All the clutter fattens with daily requests for money, which I cannot ignore and cannot afford but I can't seem to throw out.

As the clutter stacks up about me I feel powerless.

# Beware Of What You Wish For
## Nancy Humphriss

Summer was approaching, and I had just finished my first year in college. It was a requirement that I find a summer job to help pay my expenses, so I gave some thought as to what might be available. I would be living at home until the fall semester began, and I didn't have a car, so I need to find something in town. Not a lot of jobs were available with a population of only 10,000.

One thing I had accomplished in my first year was getting a lifeguard certificate, so I checked into the Parks Commission to see what might be available. The more I thought about it, the more I liked this idea. Waiting tables was low on my list of interesting work, as was selling shoelaces and underwear at the department store. So I applied, and without any further effort, I got the job. Oh joy!

While the pay wasn't great, it would do. I saw myself sitting in the sun, slowly but surely acquiring a lovely, bronzed body, which, I thought, highlighted my blue eyes and curly brown hair. I realized I would need to watch the water for any possible drownings, but it seemed that anything like that was unlikely to happen. Certainly I should be able to have some time when all seemed under control to read the latest novel or magazines on movies and fashion. Children had to be accompanied by a parent or older sibling in order to swim, so they were responsible for keeping their kids safe, too.

My post was on a small, sandy beach on a pond in one of the town's parks. Attached to the dock were two small rowboats, secured by a rope around a post. These were not pleasure boats, but there to facilitate rescues should there be a need. There was a grassy shaded area where there were several picnic tables, and a small place with restrooms and changing facilities. All seemed too good to be true, but in spite of the fact my expectations were a bit unrealistic, there didn't seem to be any flaw in my idea of having the best possible job in the world.

It all started out quite well with sunny days and happy children playing in the sand and jumping around in the warm summer water. I did know my responsibilities, so I kept watch, even while eating my peanut butter and jelly sandwiches my Mom had prepared for me. At 6:00 when the park closed the swimming area, I went around picking up used napkins, paper bags, discarded candy wrappers, and collecting forgotten towels and such.

But the day came when some teenage boys decided to "steal" the boats. Alarmed, I blew my whistle, shouted at them to return immediately, and finally ran into the water, swimming mightily after them in a fruitless attempt to catch them. They enjoyed all this immensely, laughing as I continued my efforts. Returning to the beach, I wondered what I should do now, and whether I would lose my job, since two boats were stolen on my watch. I decided that I would report this when the day was over and take the consequences. Fortunately, that never had to be, since the boys, not bad boys, really, returned the boats at the end of the day.

A few days after this, the real test came. A young girl, ten or eleven, came running up to me, crying—no, sobbing—saying, "I can't find my little brother. My mother told me to watch him while she ran some errands, but I can't find him anywhere!" I quickly surveyed the area, but no little brother could be seen.

"Maybe he went with your Mom at the last minute." I suggested. She was sure that was not the case, since he was sitting on her blanket for a while after she had left, and his clothes were still there. Becoming panicky now, I blew my whistle and instructed everybody to get out of the water so I could search around for Tim. This was a pond, not a pool, so visibility was nil as far as seeing anyone floating below the surface. With kids and dogs and people jumping around in the shallow edges, it was far too murky and dirt-filled to see anything. I then told everyone to search the area, under the picnic tables, in the bathrooms, out in the parking lot, etc. No Timmy anywhere. I told two adults to take a boat out a bit farther where the water was clear and see if they could see anything. Now I was ready to go to the changing room where there was a phone and call the police and an ambulance. I was in total panic, total despair, feeling overcome with guilt at not being more vigilant, and full of sorrow at what might be facing the parents. Some punishment for me might also be in the future, well deserved, I knew.

Then, at the height of the frenzy, we heard a loud giggle coming from somewhere overhead. Following the sound with my eyes, I could see, high up in the tree, hidden almost completely by the heavy foliage, a figure straddling a branch, with skinny little legs hanging down. Timmy! He was looking down at us, enjoying the crisis he had created, but too little to know how terrible the last few minutes had been for those below. By now his Mom had returned, and she screamed at him, half in anger, half in relief, instructing him to come down immediately.

Timmy did just that, now crying and saying he was sorry, and upon landing at his mother's feet, he was covered with hugs and kisses, not only by his mom, but by his sister, me, and others so relieved to have him safe.

There were no repercussions for me, but I did talk with the mom, apologized, and vowed to be more vigilant. Timmy's sister was reprimanded strongly, but the mother recognized that she was a bit too young to be left with such a responsibility.

It was an educational experience on several levels: I learned about assessing responsibility whenever taking on a task or job; showing maturity and recognizing reality when judging something; avoiding self-interest over fulfilling requirements; admitting wrongdoing when appropriate.

The final straw in my perfect summer job came late in August when I was a bridesmaid in a wedding. When the

Wedding Party picture was developed, most people didn't know who I was because my tan was so deep, it was unbecoming and way overdone. Tanned to a crisp! You can bet that next summer, no perfect life guard jobs for me!

# The Book with the Avocado Green Cover

Shirley Johnson

The book with the avocado green cover, with the words "Date Book" in faded gold letters, was on my bookshelf all the time. It was not lost, but had been forgotten until the other day when, looking for something else, I opened the book and found that it was a diary that started on January 1, 1945. I wrote in it fairly faithfully until August when the pages go blank. Until then, it gives me a picture of my twenty-year-old self, sixty-nine years into the past, awakening memories of a time I barely recall, and finding people who disappeared from my life long ago.

This other self and her life have taken over my present. Instead of living in the "now," I cannot stop trying to understand who I was and what people and happenings informed my days and affected the decisions I made at that important time. My handwriting is legible, but now and then, when I am about to reveal some juicy bit, I am frustrated because the words are written in shorthand. Shorthand would have prevented my roommate from reading my entry, but except for a few words, I cannot translate those now mysterious symbols I learned in a middle school classroom.

Further suggesting that these pages harbored secret material, I also sometimes wrote in French, which I was studying then. That part of the diary I can still read with ease.

More meaningful than any words are a few pictures of people I cared for at the time, and who were lost to me in the whirlwind at the end of World War II. One is a picture of me with two men in uniform who were in a program for soldiers who were to be sent to Italy after the war. I did not know it at the time, but the purpose was for them to partner with the partisans, the wartime secret underground, in rebuilding a democratic government.

My roommate, Elinor, who studied Italian, invited me to go to the Italian Club with her. There, I had wine with my dinner for the first time, and there, I met Gabriele Musatti, one of the soldiers in the picture, and by the end of the second meeting of the Italian Club, I was in love for the first time.

Recently talking with Elinor, I learned that Gabriele was from Venice, had a degree from an eastern college, and had been sent by his parents to study here before the war, probably to avoid being drafted into Mussolini's army. The strange and unsettling part of my memory is that I don't recall what he told me about himself, but I have a vivid recollection of my own deep feelings. I recorded every date we had, every call to the dorm he made, how often we went out with other people, and how I wished it would be only the two of us. When the entire group of Italians left, he called to say goodbye, and my diary records receiving his first letter, "the most beautiful I have ever had." I wish I could report that I saved it somewhere. Records show I answered the letter over a week later, and I can only wonder why I waited so long. I did find a later letter from Gabriele in which he was strongly advised me against joining the Waves. That seems strange, for I don't believe I was ever seriously considering going into any of the services.

Of course we lost touch with each other. Gabriele may have gone back to Italy where he had family and a family business. I graduated from college and went on with a life that has been a satisfying one, but I never again had a romance that was cut so short by the upheaval of the world around me, leaving me with a powerful memory of a first love.

# Neither a Borrower nor a Lender Be
### Joyce Cass

I do both and I like doing it. I borrowed some nail polish remover from my neighbor, Shirley. I lent a small vase constructed to hold a single flower to another friend. This was returned to me with a fresh new blossom in it. The whole idea of borrowing and lending for me is a warm act of sharing and gives me pleasure.

# A KWIKTAX CAPER
## Jack Russ

Last spring, in the middle of tax season, curiosity led me to ask Dad what was giving him such a bad time working on the family tax return. After all, he'd done it each year for as long as I could remember. My innocent offer to help led to an angry exchange. Dad's brief but heated reply was, "Later. I'm busy now."

Later never happened. Leaving the question in limbo proved to be another of my dumb decisions. I should have insisted. But no, not me. I'm smart. I can do that stuff any time with a little coaching. Even though the taxes looked easy when he worked, doing the taxes kept him grumpy for a month or so before annual taxes were due. I insisted I could do the taxes any time he'd let me. We had some brief discussions about him training me, going over his files and records, and eventually doing them myself when I was ready. His reply was always "Later. When we have some time. But I'm busy now. There's plenty of time." So I didn't persist. After all, it was on the computer, all organized.

Dad died suddenly, two days after Thanksgiving. A week later, the mail revealed an unexpected problem. Our family income tax report was due next April. Mom wasn't up to doing taxes, especially so soon after Dad's passing. Like it or not, the taxes had become an unwelcome challenge for me. Mom was not familiar with the computer or the taxes, for that matter. But it couldn't be that difficult. Dad had managed it well for many years. I had taken accounting in school. It appeared to be nothing to worry about. A good start, however, was to explore what was needed.

What to do next seemed fairly easy. Several things came to mind. First, dig out Dad's copy of the last year's tax report. Start by making a copy, then fill in the data with the updated values for this tax year. It sounded easy enough. Dad had kept good records, or at least I thought he had.

My next challenge: figure out where Dad had kept his figures. This not-simple challenge put an additional damper on the Christmas season. Dad's previous year's report emerged when a two-day intensive search revealed an unmarked box of papers at the top of the hall closet behind a box of shoes. Another box next to it contained the transactions for the rental property Mom and Dad had sold early January of the previous year

By New Year's I'd made some progress, but encountered a number of terms lacking definition. How or where could I find what the form asked for? Once found, what was being requested? How was the requested info determined or calculated? The list of questions grew rapidly. My anxiety level rose with it.

By mid-January, I faced a problem. Either I get someone to do the family taxes or do it myself. Maybe some expertise might help on some of the questions—especially those segments totally foreign to me. I figured if that was the case, I could do the taxes with an occasional call to Tony if needed.

I contacted Tony Davis who had been Dad's friend and was in the tax business. He was swamped with other clients, he said, but would answer some brief questions, if needed. Then Tony suggested a simple way for me to proceed. Buy a commercial software tax application called KWIKTAX. "It's easy, fast, reliable, and everyone uses it," he said. There was plenty of time. I ordered the software and awaited the promised on-screen guidance.

By mid-February, the software was in place, but using it wasn't the snap Tony had promised. He did help explain some items and terminology, but his comments were brief and often contained terms I didn't understand. In several instances, the form's question didn't seem to pertain to us. He said I could ignore them and leave the data cell blank. That was a great relief. I followed that guidance frequently thereafter.

By the beginning of April I'd followed the computer program as well as I could. Tony rejected a review of my completed report. "Swamped with other clients," he said. The deadline for the tax report was April 16th. The computer reported that I had checked all the boxes and answered all the questions, most of them, anyway. It told me my tax return was ready to file electronically. Just push the "Send" button and I was finished—and before the deadline.

Sure enough, about an hour later, there was a notification on the computer screen saying the Internal Revenue Service had acknowledge receipt of my report with the note, "Final Review Pending."

Delighted, I told my mother the good news and reported we could expect an $8,308 refund. It was finally time to celebrate.

I contacted my married older sister and invited her and her husband to join us the next weekend at the best restaurant in town to celebrate our unexpected fortune. We had a great time and shared a bottle of champagne.

Three weeks later, an envelope from the IRS was delivered asking me to complete and return the six-page IRS form 8808B in thirty days, copy attached, regarding the property Mom and Dad had sold in January last year. Unless it was received for their review within thirty days, we owed $21,300 in additional taxes.

# For Worse or For Better
Hal Peters

Don and I spent four years at Tamalpias High School in Mill Valley, California, from 1948 to 1952, but never met, not uncommon in a class of nearly five hundred and fifty students. However, several years after I'd begun working in a large sporting goods department in San Francisco, he came into the store with a mutual acquaintance and we instantly clicked as friends.

Appearance-wise, he was about five-foot-seven with a rather stocky but muscular build accented by a prominent chest expanded over time by deep breathing from a chronic asthma condition. He wore black-rimmed glasses with thick lenses and had dark brunette hair combed in a "can opener," a popular hairstyle of the day. He fit my mother's description of a "nice looking young man."

The majority of Don's early childhood and high school years were spent indoors alone, as he was an only child of two kind and caring parents, Will and Barbara Ertman. Along with his breathing difficulties, a serious eye malady had afflicted him almost from birth, greatly impairing his vision, especially distance-wise. So sports activities were impossible. In his late teens he'd undergone a rare cornea transplant and

90

suddenly a new world emerged. At last, at twenty, he was ready to pursue the pleasures he postponed for such a long time! That's where I came in. I taught him how to shoot pistols and rifles, fish for trout, and play basketball and tennis. Don truly exuded joy from every pore when participating in these new found delights!

We double-dated, and Don, an underwriter for the San Francisco Branch of Great Falls Insurance Company, consistently had an attractive female co-worker as his companion. He was easygoing, fun-loving, intelligent, respectful, and a great dancer. Finally, after dozens of casual dates, he met Sandy, a seventeen-year-old blonde, blue-eyed beauty who'd recently graduated from a Marin County high school. This Patti Page look-alike had joined the file clerks at Great Falls and quickly was "discovered" by Don.

Following an extremely brief engagement, they married in Reno, moved into an apartment in San Rafael, where all seemed fine for a few months, until Sandy quite unexpectedly proclaimed that she was unsatisfied with her position at the insurance firm. Seems her high school education had better qualified her as a bookkeeper, and her file clerk job was boring her. Fortunately, her father-in-law, an insurance adjuster, got her an accounting job at Bailey's Auto Body Shop in Oakland. She was delighted! Apparently, the pay must have been better, because within a few months, the couple moved into a roomier apartment and purchased a small boat capable of towing water skiers, Sandy's favorite pastime.

Approximately eight months to a year after

commencing with Bailey's, Don received a call from Mr. Bailey requesting his immediate presence at the Oakland facility. After obtaining permission to leave work, he swiftly drove to the East Bay business where George Bailey astounded him by accusing Sandy of embezzling thirty-two thousand dollars! The shop had been investigating losses for some time and upon questioning, Sandy had confessed to squirreling away sixteen thousand dollars in accounts in three different banks.

Will, Don's father, in an attempt to avoid jail time for his daughter-in-law, stated he would pay the proven sixteen thousand dollar loss. Sums in the three banks had been dissipated to almost zero. Tragically, Will's twenty-year mortgage had recently been paid off on his tiny San Rafael bungalow, but now he had to borrow on it once again to meet Sandy's obligation. Because of this tragic situation, Don and Sandy thought it was best to "get out of Dodge," so Don was granted a transfer to Reno, and shortly after their arrival, Sandy obtained a position in a government office in town.

Occasionally, I'd get a call from Don claiming all was going well and that they were getting back on their feet financially. They'd sold the motor boat. Prior to their departure to Nevada, their new cherry red Chevy convertible was stolen while parked outside his parents' house during the family's farewell dinner. It was recovered by the police three miles away burned to a crisp! Following father Will's advice, they'd taken the insurance reimbursement and bought an older pre-owned car, placing the extra funds in the bank.

One evening as my wife Renee and I sat chatting in our

Corte Madera home, we were interrupted by the ringing of the phone. It was Don, his voice echoing as though he were speaking from a cave or tunnel. I could instantly sense discouragement in his greeting and began the conversation by asking, "You sound as if you're calling from a tomb, Don, are you okay?" He stammered, "Sandy has left me! I'm sitting on the only piece of furniture left in the whole apartment! Everything is gone but this chair and a desk lamp. She even took my socks and underwear and most of my clothes! My guns, fishing and camping gear are gone too!"

Don told me that he hadn't a clue to any infidelity, as he and his delinquent spouse had made love the morning of the day she vanished with virtually everything but his wedding band. He was truly in a tremendous state of shock! The shock quickly turned to anger upon receiving a MasterCard statement containing evidence that Sandy and her lover financed their trip to New Jersey with the married couple's dollars. The morning after he broke the depressing news to me, he went to his wife's place of employment where the office personnel informed him that Sandy and an associate employee had been taking extended lunch hours together for months, leading co-workers to assume a serious relationship was evolving. However, they were dumbfounded when he told them they'd run away together.

My disheartened buddy remained in Reno attempting to make some semblance of order from chaos and a decent existence for himself. However, he was completely drained of trust and thoroughly depressed. The "Why me?" question was constantly on his mind. We talked often.

But about six weeks after Sandy's disappearance, I heard from Don. Wow! What a difference in the tone of his voice! Strong, confident, and self-assured!

"Guess what, Hal? The doorbell rang a few minutes ago, and when I opened the door, guess who was standing there? Sandy! She said she'd made a terrible mistake and begged for another chance. I looked her right in the eye and said, 'No more chances, Sandy. Good-bye,' and slammed the door shut."

He had applied for a divorce which was days away from being granted when she reappeared. That was the last he saw or heard from her again.

Almost a year had passed when Don was required to attend a Great Falls Insurance seminar in San Francisco. Upon returning to his meeting room after lunch, he literally bumped into another striking blue-eyed blonde. Diane, age twenty-five, was at the same hotel at a nurse's conference. She resided in a tiny town in southern Illinois and this was her first trip to a major U.S. city. She was scheduled to depart San Francisco in two days, but rearranged her travel plans after meeting Don, who had immediately asked her to dinner on the day they met.

We got an urgent call from Don during his seminar. Renee and I simply must come to the City to meet his new "Wonder Woman." He was head-over-heels in love again! Of course, we quickly arranged to meet this charmer, and we, too, fell completely in love with this sweet, kind, and thoughtful angel from mid-America. She was the complete antithesis of spouse number one.

They married, moved to the Great Falls, Montana, had Donnie Jr., and lived happily ever after!

# The Evolution of a Cook
Karin Fitzgerald

## *Lettuce*

1934

I want to get back to my first-grade class, but Mother is busy making what she calls a "lettuce snow cone." Every day I walk the few blocks home for lunch and almost every day I carefully take the pieces of lettuce out of my sandwich and leave them on the side, uneaten. Sometimes she makes a little lettuce cup, holding something good. I sneak the greens and tuck them under my plate, but my eagle-eyed mother expects this by now. She rolls the re-captured lettuce leaves into a cylinder shape, holds them together with a toothpick, sprinkles the top with sugar, and wraps this creation in a paper napkin. She hands this to me before I'm allowed to open the door. I take the lettuce cone, kiss my mother goodbye, and slowly walk until I'm out of sight of the house. Then with a little flip, I toss the hated green stuff into the gutter. Happy now, I skip along to school.

# *Peaches*

1942

The smell of peaches fills the air. Steam saturates every pore. It's canning time again. While my two younger brothers are outside having fun, I'm Mother's designated right hand helper and my job is pulling the skin off the round yellow balls as they come out of the boiling water bath. I whine to myself, *I'm a poor mistreated eight-grader; is this my future? Always the table setter, table clearer and peach-skinner. Dear God, please help me get out of this kitchen.*


# *Homemade Chocolate Pudding*

1944

I sew the ruffled pinafore that makes me look like I should be yodeling my way up the Alps and make a promise to myself that come hell or high water, I will not take the second semester of my high school "Home Ec" course, because the whole rest of the year we will be COOKING. I've heard from some of the older girls that along with mac and cheese we'll be learning how to stir up a puddle of handmade chocolate pudding. I thought you got pudding out of a box, and I don't even like chocolate. I waylay my dear old science teacher. He listens to my tale of woe and is able to finally persuade the school principal that trying to teach me to cook would be a waste of time and resources. I transfer into his wonderful biology class and spend the rest of the year doing important things, like cutting up frogs.

## *Chitlins*

1952

My darling husband walks in the door and places a large bucket of something that looks like nothing I'd want to eat on the kitchen counter. "The butcher said we should render this pig fat down and then you'll have plenty of lard for your pie crusts." He says this with a big Irish smile, and I realize that the *WE* in the rendering sentence is strictly editorial. He's taught me to make perfect pies, so I guess he figures his work is done.

With a wave and a kiss, he's off to his job. I'm still looking for one and wish I was sitting at a desk, rather than what I'm about to do. The large cast iron woodstove in our Seattle Vets' housing is still a big mystery to me, but I'm game, so I hoist the bucket of guts onto the black top, lift the round lid with a lid-lifting thing, throw small pieces of wood into the yawning opening and sit back with high expectations. Pretty quickly I'm able to scoop liquid pig fat into jars and think that this rendering business isn't so bad.

The jars are standing in a row across the drain board, slowly turning a brilliant white with cooling lard. I'm left with a funny-looking mess at the bottom of the bucket, so I lift the stove lid and throw these pig leftovers into the smoldering fire. With a *whoosh* and huge roar, part of the stovetop turns cherry red and the stovepipe shakes and howls. I realize I may burn this whole flimsy shitcan Vets' housing down if I can't stop the fire in my stove. I'm terrified. I run out the door with a bowl in my hand, scrape up snow, rush back in, and throw snow onto the flames. Back and forth I race. The fire is finally out, the floor is slick with dirty water, and splatters of congealing lard speckle the counter. Now it's time to cry. That's the way my husband finds me. "Poor, poor girl," he says, and then cleans the kitchen and the stove and restarts the fire.

## *Whole Wheat Bread*

1954

Our beautiful thirteen-month-old baby boy is sound asleep in his crib, so I pick up the big bowl of bread dough and hurry down three flights of stairs to the furnace room of this apartment house in Juneau, Alaska. The heat makes this the perfect place for bread to rise and I'm now baking two loaves once a week. The terrific bread book published by Safeway Stores is my baking bible. The pictures and instructions are so explicit an extraterrestrial could learn to bake bread. Every week or so, I try a new recipe and my repertoire increases by leaps and bounds. That warm, yummy, yeasty aroma emanating out of the kitchen, the generous slather of butter on each fresh slice. There's nothing quite like it. The satisfaction I feel when my husband and little son ask for another piece is deeply heart-warming.


## *Beef Bourguignon*


1970

The six of us are laughing at one of Joanne's outrageous jokes. We're knee-deep in delicious food and ready to serve a dinner that we've prepared for 250 people. My dear friend Joanne Kelly, a natural born cook of the splendid kind, decided to start a catering business, and it's taken off like a rocket. When she needed help, she asked me, and I'm in my second year of this temporary gig. We press gang our kids, including the boys, for lots of slicing, dicing, and prep work. Collectively, we have nine children. Right now, her two girls and my two, all teenagers, will go with us to help in the kitchen and serve. They always want to do this because it's so much fun. If Joanne and I wanted to take a break, we could turn it over to these four without a worry. I'm telling you, these girls can cook.

# *Snickerdoodles*

1986

I help my three-year-old grandson onto the stool, and he stands beside me in his funny little polar bear apron. Cookies are his favorite thing to cook, and I hand him the bowl with two large eggs. He confidently cracks the eggs on the side of the bowl, and he's ready to use his little flour sifter for the dry ingredients. I think back to our first egg-breaking lesson and smile to myself.

On that day, I have a dozen eggs in the carton and I show him how to hold the egg, tap it on the side of the bowl with one hand, then use both thumbs to pull the shell apart. He's timid at first, and worried about breaking something so perfect-looking. *Crack, Crack, Crack,* one by one, the eggs slide into the bowl, a little shell here and there, but that would be something for a later lesson. When the twelfth egg plops into the bowl, he's laughing and hopping up and down. I feel a huge sense of delight in his feelings of accomplishment. It was as if I knew that one day this first-born grandchild would become a chef.

# *Chili*

1993

Snow is blurring the windows, but it's not a real Alaskan blizzard yet. All four kids, grownups now, and their kids are hanging out; a ping pong game is going full blast downstairs, while a tired group upstairs is either reading or sleeping on the giant bed we've named the "Passion Pit," with its bank of pillows in the alcove.

We all treasure these get-togethers. With such busy lives, it doesn't happen very often. Our ski cabin has been the scene of so many delicious meals, and tonight we'll share everyone's favorite after-ski dish. It's a little specialty of mine I call "Granny K's Killer Chili." The name sounds like it could sizzle your tongue, but it's really not that hot. I've seen my adult children hold the huge pot I use for this chili, and when I think it's empty, they will use a spatula in order to scrape out every last morsel. Then rounding out the menu, we'll have tri-color coleslaw with jalapeño cornbread on the side. I sometimes feel like an archeologist when I make "Will's Three-Berry Pie" for dessert. It took me two years of gentle but persistent digging to finally have this chef on the Oregon coast give up his secret recipe. Tradition then demands that we play a game of "Hearts" after dinner. It's fang and claw because the stakes are so high. The loser has to wash the dishes. It's not all bad news because the LOSER gets to choose one of the fellow card players who must dry the dishes and put them away. It's ruthless, super fun, and no one is safe.

## *Meat Loaf Surprise*

2004

Sometimes just saying the name of something jogs a wonderful memory, but sometimes that word or phrase evokes an instant recollection of an event so unpalatable you don't even want to hear it said. Here's what happens in my family when "Meat Loaf Surprise" is mentioned: giggles and guffaws and pantomimed gagging from the four Fitzgerald/Amodios. I can't blame them; they were there.

It was a cooking lesson gone terribly wrong. The format for my volunteer cooking program with my grandkids was one lesson a week for four weeks. We would prepare a whole dinner and the parents would come to my house and dine, or the food would be taken to their home. I loved to try new dishes and found this interesting recipe for a meat loaf that looked like a jelly roll. My granddaughter, Madeleine Amodio, was an enthusiastic *sous chef* and embarking on her lesson, she bravely patted out a rectangle of seasoned uncooked hamburger onto a sheet of parchment. She and I then debated how much of the special ingredient, called "Greek caviar" we should spread on top of the meat. The recipe's instructions said a thin layer of this Kalamata olive spread, but I sometimes feel if one teaspoon is good, then two must be better. Maddy was unconvinced, but I was the executive chef, so we used the whole jar of Greek Caviar. The final topping was a layer of shredded mozzarella cheese. We both admired how perfect the loaf looked when it was rolled up.

By the time Maddy's mom, (my youngest daughter, Debra) her dad, Tom, and young brother, Bennett, arrived, the Meat Loaf Surprise was ready to serve. I regretted that my husband and I had an invitation to another dinner and wouldn't be able to share in this meal. What happened next is embedded in family history. Daughter Debra described the scene: Son-in-law Tom cut four generous slices of the meat loaf and my daughter said it looked too dangerous to eat. "The thick, black glistening circle of Kalamata olives surrounded by the ring of brown hamburger, and the center filled with oozing, melted, pale yellow mozzarella cheese. Bennett wanted to go home, but Maddy argued that we should at least try a bite." Her voice dropped to a whisper, "Mom, it was truly the worst thing any of us had ever eaten."

The wretched mess was put in the garbage and their family finished the evening at a local restaurant. My son-in-law, Tom, a lawyer, said he thought they might be able to have me charged with child endangerment or maybe attempt to do grave bodily harm. This legal *bon mot* deserved a weak chuckle from me. I felt bad that I'd doubled up on the ingredients, and especially sorry for Maddy. She had such high hopes. And me, well I *mea culp*'ed all over the place and lost some of my cooking creds for a while.

## Pineapple Fried Rice

2014

Here I am, a permanent snow bird. "California here we come," that's what we said when Alaskan winters weren't fun anymore and we moved to Santa Rosa five years ago. My darling Fitzy, gone now after almost 61 years of marriage, was the real reason that I learned to cook and that I enjoy it so much. He was such a game guy, always ready to try anything I stirred up. The purple halibut cooked in red wine by mistake, the curried shrimp overdosed with too much curry, the bright green mashed potatoes on St. Patrick's Day. I could write a book about my cooking experiments and his encouragement and good humor.

Our favorite cuisine was Thai, but I'd never tried to prepare it before. I know that Fitzy would have loved this new phase in my personal cooking journey. Back from an all-day Thai cooking lesson in San Francisco, I invite my California kids and grandkids (half of my family is still living in Alaska) to a Thai dinner, cooked by me. I start with mini chicken satays in peanut sauce, little fresh summer rolls with spicy lime soy sauce, and Thai glazed cashews (that are so addictive the Thai cooking instructor said she has to hide these from her husband). All the while, we're sipping Green Iguana cocktails. The kids are drinking organic apple juice with bright green straws. The meal is served buffet style: a small salad of spicy Thai cukes and pineapple fried rice served in hollowed-out pineapple shells. I can't help myself; I've added delicious shrimp to this dish. My family *oohs* and *ahs* and I can't stop beaming because this dinner is KILLER. I thank you, family, and thank you, Fitzy. It's great to know that I've still "got it".

Bon Appetite.

# Waiting and Patience
### Dorothy Herbert

It depends on what I am waiting for to gauge my patience in the process.

If it is the arrival of loved ones, I wait impatiently.

If it is the arrival of the Man with the Scythe,

I can wait patiently for an eternity.

I have less patience with my declining abilities.

Why can't I do it and do it now?!

For little ones who are still finding their way,

I have great patience.

For older ones who believe their way is the only way

and demand that others follow it,

my patience has a short fuse.

Is patience an offshoot of understanding?

# Visual Puns
## Bernice Schachter

Forty years of my life was devoted to hard labor at many stone carving studios. The unexpected consequence was that I found joy in being immersed in stone dust. Even the cacophony of the noisy equipment always sounded like music to my deaf ears.

Two years ago I started to write my legacy for my great-grandchildren yet-to-be. It is about how, why, and what inspired me to create over 400 sculptures. Now I am left only with the photos and the memories. Some of my works were broken or bartered, sold or stolen, or given away to friends and family. Since I have had my first great-granddaughter, I am ready to finish writing *My Legacy in Stone*. It will detail feelings about my life choices and how and what influenced my work. It is not a chronological memoir, but an explanation of how I expressed ideas, emotions, desires, and thoughts in my sculptures. I divided the book into twelve different chapters based on the series I grouped together in a body of work. Each of these chapters will tell something about my life and the inspiration for the sculptures.

Creating them helped me live my life to the fullest. In my final years, I miss the challenge of living the three-dimensional life of discovery, dedication, and discipline. The following is an excerpt from the book:

I began this group of sculptures I call "Visual Puns" in the Fall of 1994, after carving for twenty-four summers in Pietrasanta, Italy. Once I stopped working in Europe, I moved my workshop for sculpture to Fountain Valley, California. I joined a group of professional sculptors who invested their time and money to set up a studio for serious stone carvers. Those attending were many of my students who had worked with me previously in Italy.

This new body of work demonstrated an encounter with materials other than marble, and the discovery of a new personal imagery. It was a departure from my usual style of direct carving. I gave myself permission to have fun and play with fragments of marble of various shapes and colors, and, in some instances, combining them with stainless steel components and Lucite. The natural textures, colors, and shapes of the stone were an integral part of the composition. Each piece was arrived at playfully, intuitively, and instinctively, culminating in an idea without preconception. Elation and joy were the result of finding a meaning for each of these pieces as I looked for something that would clue me into an inspiration for each work.

The "Visual Puns" were created with the intention to have the viewer discover what the sculptures were about and what they were meant to convey. The title of the work gave clues to what I wanted to express. For example, several pieces of alabaster I carved were a series of knots. When I was asked why I was doing so many knots, I replied, "Why not?" So I entitled this group "Why Knots."

"Rock Star" is a double entendre depicting Elton John on one side and a white marble star set into the green marble on the backside.

"Desert Storm" was a timely piece representing a weapon of destruction during the Gulf War period.

"Past Times" and "Sacred Steps" indicated the ideas came from other cultures.

"Gemini" represented the duality of twins by duplicating parts in acrylic.

"What Goes Around" combined a stainless steel wheel set into the green marble. Unfortunately, this piece needed a change in title after the great earthquake of 1994. I reassembled the broken parts and renamed it "Northridge."

My work defined me as a woman and holds my memories of times past, my role models, my sorrows, and great satisfaction in what I created. It is my hope that the family's next generation will be creative and find great joy in whatever they choose to do in their lifetime.

*Legacy in Stone* will be dedicated to Leila Gray Varon born June 24, 2014.

# Blind Date
## Nikki King

In late September of 1956 I had just moved to San Francisco with two Mills College classmates following my June graduation. Shortly after arriving, my friend who lived nearby called to ask if I was interested in a blind date with a law student from the University San Francisco.

"Sure I'm interested" I replied enthusiastically. My goal had always been to date a law student or a lawyer, mainly because in those days, law students were usually liberal in their thinking and I was an enthusiastic Adlai Stevenson Democrat. In addition, my father and grandfather were lawyers, and I greatly admired that profession.

That evening my blind date arrived (after climbing the two sets of stairs to reach my apartment door). He was an attractive guy. Tall and well-built with clear blue eyes, he gave the impression that he was at ease and confident within himself. I felt very comfortable with him immediately. My mouth was numb from that day's experience at the dentist and his eyes were blurry after a recent eye exam. Nevertheless, our first impressions of each other were extremely favorable! We clicked immediately.

Eight months later, we were married and this June we celebrated our 57th anniversary!

# Dare to Be a Bubble
Sally Tilbury

In 1975, my husband was the chairman of the American Society of Travel Agents convention. There had been more than 4,000 participants from all areas of the travel industry, including delegates from airlines, hotels, travel publications and other related industries. The major convention was held in Rio and the delegates later fanned out to destinations within South America.

When the convention was over, my husband and I arranged to go to Iguassu from Rio to see Iguassu Falls spill out of forests where rivers converge at the corner of Brazil, Argentina, and Paraguay. People disagree as to whether the Brazilian side of the falls is more spectacular than the Argentinian side. We chose the Brazilian side and accommodations at the *Hotel Cataratas*, located within walking distance of the falls.

Bus time from the airport through the tropical rainforest was long and bumpy. "Count me out of these humid adventures," I thought as I fanned myself in the non-air-conditioned bus. First we tried opening the windows, but found the jungle was hotter and buggier than inside the bus, so we closed them abruptly, shutting out the buzzy, bugging noise and bird chatter of the jungle. We continued to thump along in the breathless air when suddenly, we heard a mysterious clashing sound and the bus burst into a clearing.

There was our luxurious hotel in the middle of a park-like setting. The hotel was a colonial style mansion. I was most interested in its advertised air conditioning. It was to be our oasis in the jungle. We walked to the overlook to see the falls whose noise was thumping in our ears.

The Falls of Iguassu are the widest in the world, as wide as three Niagaras and one hundred feet higher. They split into 275 inlets and drops, making it far more complex than Niagara. The initial drop of Angel Falls is exactly half a mile. Spray gathers in a rockfall at the bottom to form a second plunge. The total fall, 3,212 feet, is the highest on earth. This creates a booming sound of pounding water and makes clouds of spray endlessly going, "*Pshh, pshh, pshh.*" We could hear the pounding and crashing all night from our hotel room.

It never stops, this crashing water, all day and night, far louder than angry ocean surf. During daylight hours, there was also the "*flop/flop*" noise of the rotor blades of two helicopters flying tourists for close-up views of the falls. As one tiny helicopter landed, the other became airborne.

Then came the spontaneous decision: a response to a dare. One of the tiny helicopters hovered and came in for a landing near us. The helicopter took only one passenger. It was an *either/or* challenge. Just as well. The children would miss us. Chuck thought it would be great fun if I took the ride into the Falls. "Everyone does it," he said. "When will you ever get a chance like this?"

Where was my caution?

The helicopter steadied itself, stopped swaying, and landed. I stepped in, just like that. My first discovery was that the pilot was young and handsome and spoke but a little English. My next discovery was that there was no shoulder harness, only a lap belt. That made sense inasmuch as there was no inner structure in this bubble to affix a seat belt.

How do you say "Help!" in Portuguese?

The controls and panel were only in front of the pilot, leaving no place to brace myself. I looked at the view to the right, left, from between my knees, and beyond my ankles. Such is the view from inside a bubble. We took off vertically as helicopters do. It was then I remembered I had been in a helicopter just once and regretted it the first time. Too late; we were airborne, slipping sideways.

Throughout the flight I found I could handle forward and upward, but not slipping sideways. Above all, I dreaded the dropping down part. During the more nightmarish moments when the spray hit the bubble, I closed my eyes and said, "I'm not here." This is something I made up as a child to combat car sickness.

I clutched the seat itself, relying only on the lap belt and my grip on the seat for support when the handsome pilot banked. Again I looked for a strap, but no, this machine was as much Plexiglas as a bubble can be with the least fuselage and still function. We think it was an H-47.

114

I think my inner gyro was off. Here I was, a perfectly sensible mother of three, hovering with Agent 007 over the most awesome sight of my life and terrified. I had put my life in the hands of this handsome stranger with his awkward English. Over the sound of the crashing water, he said, "We go in the mist?" I must have nodded. Surely he would not fly us into the actual force of the spray, but there we were, hovering below the lip of the falls in the layer of mist on top of the spray. We fluttered upward, dropped down, and flitted sideways like a hummingbird. Small rainbows danced around us. I felt like an airsick Tinker Bell.

Finishing his last trick, which entailed flying through the hollow space between the falling water and the rock face, he indicated we were going back to the landing pad. I sensed my knuckles relaxing their hold on the seat. Tiny tourists became larger in my view as they stood on the overlook. Now it was time to regain my poise and look blasé in front of my gleeful husband.

Never again, A hot air balloon, OK. A Ferris wheel, maybe, but never again a dancing bubble. Ever.

*Iguacu means "Great Waters." Iguacu is one of those names spelled several ways. In English, there are two different variations: Iguasu and Iguassu. In Argentina, it is spelled "Iguazu," and in Paraguay, it is spelled "Yguazu." The Brazilian spelling is "Iguacu," pronounced "Ig-gwa-soo."*

*from **Brazil on Your Own**, Arnold Greenberg, Passport Books.*

# Bibifax
Elisabeth Levy

I am called Bibifax and I am a workaholic. My colleagues and I are taken for granted by our owners, and most of the time, we are not treated very gently. We work 24/7 and are expected to always deliver perfect results. We are supposed to work tirelessly and heaven caves in should we ever make a mistake.

I am old now and on the brink of retiring. In my younger days it was amusing to jump over letters, quickly change this and that, and see the surprised eyes of my new owner, who behaved like a schoolgirl with a new toy. She was suspicious, though, and didn't trust me. It made me laugh. She got frustrated very quickly and frequently sent e-mails to other owners she seemed to know, whom she called her rescuers. Eventually, she got used to me, and we had a relatively quiet time with only occasional upsets.

I got older and she did too. I began to slow down, whereas she used and overused me more and more and wasn't very patient. I tried to make her realize she needed to slow down, too. It was in vain. She always punches too many keys at one time. I know my reaction is not that fast anymore. I send my little beautiful rainbow-colored wheel out telling her to slow down. This has the opposite effect; she punches more keys. She doesn't seem to understand I am old, I need patience to function, and actually do a reasonably good job, considering my age.

The crowning blow came a few days ago. She is on a new project with another owner and needed to make corrections. I tried to warn her to let me warm up first. She didn't pay any attention. She punched so many keys I could not keep up with her. It took me a long time to figure out which letters she needed. Slowly, painfully, I was able to produce one after another, except sometimes she punched them so fast, I forgot which letters she wanted. I got confused, what did she want me to do? I tried to make her realize I needed some rest. 24/7 speed is out of the question now. I think eventually she sensed it. My owner is lucky. These other owners she calls rescuers always seem to help her. She turned me off for the night, and with a sigh of relief, I was able to rest.

The next morning she woke me up. It seemed she had changed her attitude. I think she was told that I was old and needed patience. First she looked and noticed what I had tried to convey to her all along. She waited until I was ready. We worked together for a while, slowly and methodically, and then she let me rest. I appreciated the pause and when she came back, we did the same. I believe she realized she had to let me rest every so often to get her desired result. We did that a few times. It worked! Gently, she changed a word, a letter at a time, and eventually, we arrived at the end of what she called a chapter. It was also the end of the day and we had accomplished what we set out to do.

I know sooner or later she won't want me anymore. What will happen to me?

# A Singular Sympatico Sunday
## Joyce Cass

Seated and sated she switched sides
Squinting straight through the slats
Seeing swallows swooping and singing
While seeking their suppers.

It was a sun-sweetened Sunday
That she started her sojourn serenely and
silently
Surveying the scene of
Songbirds seizing and sampling
Salvageable substances for survival.

After a sufficiently scrupulous session of study
Signs of sedentary self-indulgence set in
The sky-sightings became slow and scarce
Seemingly her subjects were scattering
Searching for more salubrious savories.

Surely she should be somewhat sensible
Sitting here in her secure senior sanctuary
Scanning the scenery while not satisfied.

Suddenly a serious solution submerged
Susan's selection of the "Seasons" scenarios!!
Seemed the superlative ending to Sunday's
sloth.

Self-discipline and strength became self-evident
Stiffly she stood, separating servitude to
Some semblance of significant seriousness.

As her sluggard's solitary situation was solved
Her spirits spiraled
Stimulating some sense of salient sanity
Stopping her spellbound surveillance of
Sunday's soaring and scintillating swallows.

# A Short Love Story
## Judith Klausner

As the horses reached the gate, Jonathan asked, "Do you have a sister at home just like you?"

Sarah shook her head, a dimpled smile revealing perfect white teeth. Her Hazel eyes, flecked with gold, or so it seemed to him, sparkled with gaiety, or was it mischief? She was self-conscious enough to blush. He couldn't remember the last time he saw a woman blush. Her skin was smooth and her face tanned by the New Mexico sun. Her hair, a color he could only describe as autumn leaf, was pulled back from her face and twisted in a French braid. He wondered how she could manage to keep it in place.

Jonathan didn't take his eyes off her as she watched twelve magnificent fillies run in The Santa Fe Handicap. By the time the horses had crossed the finish line, Jonathan was in love with her, even though she was married. There was no way he wanted to talk himself out of it.

In the next race, Sarah bet on the number two horse. It came in dead last. She pointed to the filly. It was limping. "Do you think 'Robin Bee' is faking that limp?" She laughed.

"She's probably afraid she won't get her oats without an excuse for bringing up the rear. Poor little filly."

So far Sarah had lost her allotted two dollars on every race. She really didn't care a fig about horses. From where Sarah sat just outside the Jockey Club at the Santa Fe Downs, she could see the track, the duck pond in the center, and the mountains beyond. Marshmallow clouds hovered over the Sangre Cristo Range. The sky today was one of New Mexico's celebrated blues, azure, with the white puffs moving slowly, dwindling away in a blanket of white like one of Georgia O'Keeffe's cloud paintings.

Sarah thought about the painting she'd started this morning. She wanted it to look like the sky clearing after a sudden storm. Maybe with a rainbow. Or perhaps, she thought, a double rainbow touching at the arch, spreading in two, blending into the purple wild flowers peppered over the pinioned mountains.

"Look, Sarah," Jonathan pointed at the duck pond, scattering her thoughts, "Look at that love scene."

A fat, male duck was waddling furiously after his female counterpart. She led him a merry chase right onto the race track. There she stopped, waiting for him to catch up with her. He approached, flapping his wings and quacking loudly, sounding like the honk of a goose. The fat male tried to mount her unsuccessfully as she flapped her wings in annoyance. The spectators began clapping, shouting words of encouragement to the frustrated fowl. A man seated behind Sarah shouted "Hey, Donald, she's just like my wife: a real prick teaser!" Sarah blushed and Jonathan laughed.

A cowboy, in full regalia astride a pinto, rode quickly to them and shooed the ducks back into the water.

"Oh my God," Sarah laughed. "That was so funny."

Jonathan pushed his sixties-style straw hat back from his forehead. His blue eyes were filled with tears of laughter. "Wow! What a show." The freckles on his nose and cheeks were the same color as his soft, wavy hair that snuck out from under the brim of his hat.

"Where did you get the straw bowler?" Sarah asked.

"Like it?"

"It's cute. It suits you. You look like a river boat gambler."

"It's Daniel's. If you like it, I'll swipe it from him."

Sarah reached for her iced tea. She felt relaxed. Daniel and Carol, Sarah's good friends from New York, had brought their friend Jonathan, a music professor from Yale, with them. He was looking for someone to go to the races with him. Carol and Daniel found they had an afternoon rehearsal for the opera, so they couldn't go. Sarah volunteered. In the sixth race, Jonathan's horse, at eight-to-one odds, won. He gave Sarah an excited hug. After the seventh race, he handed her a winning ticket. "Here's a present. I feel sorry for you; you're such a loser." They laughed.

The eighth and final race, Jonathan bet on "Wishful Thinking," bred out of "Three wishes" and "I'm Dreaming." He knew he couldn't lose. But he did.

They stood to leave. Jonathan rolled the losing ticket between his thumb and index finger for a few seconds, reluctantly tore it in half, and dropped it into an ashtray.

"Hey, Sarah, how about having a drink somewhere? You'll have to name the place." He took a chance and added, "Let me take you out to dinner, too. Carol and Daniel won't be back from the opera until late. They told me the opera doesn't start here until eight."

Sara thought for a second. Jonathan made her feel like an attractive woman. Maybe she shouldn't have come with him. "Sounds good to me. It will be an unexpected pleasure."

# Celebration
## Nikki King

On May 24th, 1987, the Golden Gate Bridge was 50 years old. To honor the occasion, the city of San Francisco organized a festive celebration. On that anniversary day, the bridge was to be closed to car traffic and pedestrians were allowed full access to the entire bridge. I decided it would be great fun to "walk the bridge" for that event.

To prepare for my adventure, I arose at 5:00 a.m. and headed to the all-night donut shop where I was meeting a friend, drank several cups of coffee, and proceeded to the bridge. By the time we arrived, a large crowd had already gathered and surged forward, pushing through the barricade 30 minutes before the scheduled starting time of 6:00 a.m. My friend and I joined the throng and were soon caught up in the excitement and thrill of the moment.

The weather was perfect—sunny with a strong breeze—the view breathtaking, and the Art Deco structure of the bridge up close was impressive in its graceful beauty. After about 15 minutes, we reached the center of the bridge, but found ourselves blocked by people approaching us from the opposite side, which ended at Marin County, 1.7 miles away from our S.F. entry point.

We were literally jammed together on all sides. Movement of any kind was next to impossible. In addition, the pressure of all those bodies created a claustrophobic, heated, closed-in atmosphere. I could feel myself starting to panic, but I convinced my friend to ease slowly through the crowd to reach the edge of the bridge directly above the water where we could breathe in the cool air more easily. As we hung onto the side railing, my friend and I started to sing old love songs to distract ourselves and fight off the panic!

After a short time, I realized I had an urgent need—the early morning coffee had moved through my system. I had no choice but to release my burden where I stood. I then distanced myself from the puddle.

"It serves them right for botching up this whole event," I thought to myself. Later, we watched a few desperate men walking *outside* of the bridge railing, holding onto the external structure. They proceeded slowly and carefully, and must have reached the end of the bridge safely, as miraculously, there were no deaths reported.

Suddenly, we heard a loud thunderous clap of noise and felt the bridge floor flatten under out feet. For a few seconds, I thought the bridge was collapsing. I learned later that the weight of all those people had caused the collapse of the normal convex shape of the bridge roadway surface, but the structure still remained sound. To reassure myself, I thought that 300,000 people couldn't possibly weigh more than hundreds of cars. I was wrong. The combined weight of those hundreds of peoples *exceeded* the traffic weight of bumper-to-bumper traffic on the bridge.

After about one and a half hours, the crush of bodies began to ease up, and we were able to walk slowly back to the entrance of the bridge and reach land. Due to the mob of people, no busses were able to reach the bridge, so we were forced to walk two miles until we reached my friend's apartment, where I collapsed and waited for my husband to rescue me.

What a terrifying experience! What a blessing that everyone on the bridge that day remained calm. There was no panic. There were no fights, heart attacks, or deaths reported. It was as if every person realized their best chance to remain safe was to be calm and still. I attribute this orderly conduct to the spirit of the Bay Area: stalwart and resilient. I guess I proved myself to be a true Californian that day!

# The Gold Ring
## Leona Biddle

*Scrunch, scrunch.* German tanks roll over crusted ice. Troops stomp along behind, coats white with frost, their breath making dense clouds as powdered snow rises like a mist from scuffling boots. It is the coldest winter on record, biting cold, so cold the fjords between Norway and Denmark's islands are frozen over. An eerie sight. So cold, we shiver in our worn coats and mended mittens, inside.

I'm curled up under a warm blanket, my nose deep in a book of Hans Christian Andersen, wrapped in a fairy tale. Mother says, "I want you to come with me."

"Where to?"

"Just put your woolen scarf and socks on and come with me. We are going downtown to run some errands."

Downtown is a twenty-minute fast walk from our house. As I get my things, my mind races. Where are we going? What can we buy? Someone sent money? Should I ask?

Mother moves quickly, determined, toward our unknown destination. The streets are icy, slick, coated with hoarfrost crunching underfoot. Even with rubber-soled wooden shoes, it is hard not to skid along. I reach up to grab Mother's elbow, but she shrugs it off. Shivering, I think the cold must be biting her, too. We proceed steadily on and on toward our destination. I wonder where we're going.

When we reach downtown, we stop in front of a jewelry store. She turns to me, her tall ten-year-old, and gazes into my eyes, blue like hers. "You must never tell Father, promise me."

I nod, puzzled.

*Ring-a-ling-a-ling.* We enter.

Inside the store, a dazzling display of sparkling rings, gold bracelets, necklaces, and watches are all spread out for the German soldiers' pleasure. Mother sighs, walks up to the counter, removes her gold wedding ring. "How much?"

Oh no. She can't do that! How can I stop her?

A slender, well groomed saleslady takes the gold band, weighs it in her hand. "It's very light." She looks at it close-up, turns, and weighs it in a miniature scale. "All I can give you is 100 *kroner.*"

Mother sighs again. "I'll take it." The money is counted out in crackling new 10 *kroner* bills. Mother carefully tucks them into her handbag. Outside, she says, "You must never tell Father that I sold my wedding ring. I lost it, remember?" I nod.

"Now we must look for a Christmas tree. He would want us to keep up the *Jule* traditions. I think last year's candles will do another year," she says out loud to herself.

We find the Christmas tree stand and Mother bargains for a small tree. The man can see we are poor by our worn, thin coats and wooden shoes, not boots. It's clear we can't pay much. "Make it 5 *kroner*." It is a beautiful little fir tree. Maybe, just maybe, it will be Christmas after all.

Maybe we will have enough *kroner* to purchase little gifts for everyone and a small goose. Maybe even apple cake with whipped cream. Mother stops at the bookstore, and I wait outside with our tree. Hand wrapped around the middle of the sticky tree trunk, I smell the pine needles squashed under my glove. Maybe I will get a book this year. She stops twice more and we walk home quickly, smiling inside, steps lightened by new hope. A real Christmas once again.

The goose will be bought the day before Christmas at a discount. The tree will be decorated with glass bells & balls, homemade paper hearts in red & white, tinsel, and lastly, the candles, lit on Christmas Eve. All of us, except Father, who is in a prisoner-of-war-camp in Hamburg, will join hands and walk around the glowing tree, singing carols. I'll notice Mother's eyes are moist, but she'll look content. It is Christmas, after all. She will whisper to me, "Remember, never tell your Father."

# Four Crashes and You're Out
Hal Peters

velyn Johnson was eighty-two in 1992 when her SOS call came to us. Her knees were telling her it was time to vacate her Santa Rosa apartment where the bathroom was on the second floor. What did we think she should do?

She'd met my mom on a double date in 1928 and they'd become lifelong friends. We'd kept in contact since my mom's passing nine years earlier and I'd known her all my life. There had been several promising relationships in her life, one a marriage proposal that was squashed by a grandfather who warned her not to marry a Catholic, a decision she deeply regretted the rest of her life. Evelyn's only relative was a nephew living in Phoenix who was having financial difficulties, thus we were "it".

Shortly after her call, we drove from our home in the Salinas Valley and hauled her meager belongings to a mobile home in the town of Salinas. The home had three short entry steps, which her knees seemed to climb easily. It was walking distance from grocery stores, restaurants, and all necessities, and was well-kept and efficiently run. She made wonderful friends there. My wife and I visited Evelyn two to three times weekly and kept up her home and yard. She truly appreciated all our efforts and was always joyful and positive.

For the elderly, "independence" is driving their own automobile. Evelyn's was a 1969 light green Chevrolet Impala. No plastic on this baby! It was designed and constructed like an armored car! Miss Johnson cared for it like the child she never had. All services were completed exactly on time and the Chevy was always detailed immaculately with true love and pride by me.

Evelyn, a professional ballerina in her youth, unfortunately was now carrying 185 pounds on her 5'7" frame. No easy job on her arthritic knees, so she literally drove everywhere. Three years after her move, her local optometrist referred her to an eye specialist in San Jose. We drove her to appointments 75 miles away. Each visit resulted in a new prescription, but she always complained there were of little help. When we questioned the doctor, he informed us that he'd done all that he could to improve her vision, but never discussed the cause of her impairment.

Shortly after her final San Jose appointment, she had the first of her three car crashes. Number one was a "head on," totally destroying the old Chevy's metal grill. The next two were less violent, but both caused major damage and were also her fault. Each time she was turning and stated that she didn't see the vehicle she hit. Fortunately, all accidents occurred at low speeds and though her "tank" destroyed several cars, miraculously, no one involved was ever injured. And strangely enough, those victims of her carelessness were always polite and respectful, and never showed anger at the crash scenes. It was apparently the "sweet old lady" syndrome, where Evelyn was merely a victim of circumstance!

Miss Johnson was insured by AAA. My wife and I met with their top executives in the Salinas office where we pleaded with them to cancel her insurance so she'd no longer be a hazard on the local roads. They calmly announced that she had been a loyal customer for over 30 years and they certainly could not in good conscience cancel her policy after such enduring loyalty! After this meeting, which was not disclosed to Evelyn, we offered to reimburse her for taxi fares to any destination of her choice, but she assured us that she'd learned her lesson and would be extremely cautious in the future.

The severity of her eyesight difficulties were graphically revealed to us when we accompanied her to the DMV to get her license renewed. When presented with the written exam, she couldn't read the questions. Incredibly, they told her that since Evelyn lived only three blocks from their office, they'd send an agent to read her the test and she could answer them orally. They came, and she never missed a question! Next was the eye test and a driving exam.

My wife and I were leaving town for an extended period and asked Evelyn to wait for our return so we could all go to the DMV together, especially since she seemed greatly concerned about the two additional tests. As was her *modus operandi*, she'd applied for her renewal more than a month before it was due, so she was still driving legally.

To our surprise and dismay, Evelyn explained the following scenario upon our return. She decided to drive herself to the DMV and take the tests without us, a typical example of her need for independence. While diagonally parking in the DMV lot, she backed into a parked car! Aware of her dilemma, a "nice man" guided her safely into a parking spot and, noting her nervousness, gallantly took her arm and assisted her up the stairs into the DMV office. Evelyn was about to thank him for his kindness as they entered the office, but before the words could leave her mouth he loudly asked, "Does anyone own a white Toyota Corolla? This lady just backed into it!"

Indeed, the owner was the DMV employee who was to give Miss Johnson her driver's exam! Instead of implementing the test, he got permission to drive the "Green Bomb" to Evelyn's home and park it in the car port, where it remained until I sold it a few weeks later.

The AAA lost a loyal customer, the streets of Salinas became considerably safer, and its taxis enjoyed Miss Johnson's company.

# Question
### Dorothy Herbert

Where is the Past located?

On an old calendar?

In my mind?

In the collective mind of friends and family?

In the great void before I was born?

It has no one location, but oozes in and out of our memories.

It has no one location, but floats in and out of the

backs of our minds, wherever those are located.

Some neurons seem to have captured it,

But too often they fade away before we can establish it.

The past floats like a leaf on a pond or stream.

# Client Care
## Jack Russ

Last Saturday, a new gold-colored Lexus sedan drove up and parked in front of the showroom here at the dealership. I suspected it might be her. It looked like the new one she bought about a month ago. I wondered what problem Mrs. Clark had encountered this time. And since I was the salesman she bought the car from, I knew she'd be expecting me to come out, greet her, and see what needed attention.

Mrs. Betsy Clark, or "The Rich Widow," as she was known by the others in the dealership, had bought a new Lexus each year for the five years I worked there, and at least each of the two years before that. She picked a different color each time and paid the asking price in cash. She insisted that I be the one she dealt with on each visit. Most of her visits were regarding minor items, explanations—again—on how some features worked, minor adjustments like resetting the mirrors, and always a free car wash and interior vacuum. We also filled the gas tank for her each visit as the manager's goodwill gesture to a good and consistent customer.

Mrs. Clark stopped the car immediately in front of the main entry, blocking it as she had done on her previous visits.

I opened the driver's door for her, helped her out, pulled her cane out for her, escorted her into the customer lounge, and parked the car nearby clear of traffic. She had become accustomed to the free coffee in the lounge and was enjoying a cup as I returned.

Before I could inquire about her needs for the car, she said, "Harry, it still rattles. You didn't fix it right the last time. I want it fixed now. I'm tired of that irritating noise."

In fairness to Mrs. Clark, she was right. We hadn't removed whatever it was that was rattling and annoying her as she drove. We couldn't identify anything. After all, the car had less than 600 miles on it. I had driven the car and couldn't identify the irritating sound she insisted she heard "whenever I go over a bump, or a rough section of road. I don't hear it on a smooth road."

I offered to take her on a road test. Perhaps I could identify what caused the mystery. She agreed and finished her coffee. I helped her into the passenger side and placed her cane safely, then went around and entered the driver's side. I looked around the seat and the floor to see if anything was loose or if anything obvious was causing the rattle. Nothing was noted. No unusual sounds were evident when the car started.

Seat belts were fashioned, but before I pulled out of the parking area, she reached across, pointed to the driver's door and said, "Hand me my sunglasses, please. They're in the door pocket. I always drive with my sunglasses during the day." I handed her the glasses case, a metallic variety I hadn't seen before. "Okay," she said.

We drove over some local roads, a couple miles on the freeway, and back to the dealership. We turned off the music to be sure nothing would interfere with any sound we might detect. Neither of us heard any unusual noises.

Upon our return to the dealership, we parked next to the service entry. I had Jake, the suspension specialist, put the car on a lift and explore under the car. He found nothing. One of the other mechanics pulled the left front wheel off just on the chance that something had come loose or perhaps an adjustment was called for. They assured Mrs. Clark that all was as it should be.

On a hunch, I asked Mrs. Clark to let me take the car out without her to see if I could locate the source of the random rattle she had encountered. I promised to be back in fifteen minutes or less. She agreed, and sat in the lounge to await my return.

When settled in the car and ready to test once more, I noted her glasses case still on the passenger seat. I returned it to the utility compartment in the lower panel of the driver's door, and headed out to a section of nearby road well known by the shop's workmen as a demanding auto suspension test bed.

The test took at most five minutes before the car was returned to the dealer's site, the culprit in hand.

Jake fashioned a shallow sponge rubber insert to the driver's door utility compartment. Hereafter, the glasses case would no longer slide around or rattle whenever the car experienced a rough road or sudden stop.

Mrs. Clark left the showroom, her car freshly washed, and with a full tank of gas.

# Mama Goes to the Bronx
Judith Klausner

Bessie sat in her overstuffed blue chair. Her rinsed hair was a shade lighter than the upholstery. Penciled-on eyebrows zoomed off her forehead at rakish angles, and the old woman's crimson lips formed a ruler-perfect line that disappeared into deep wrinkles on the sides of her mouth.

Bessie's thin arms ended in blue-veined hands and arthritic fingers. She clutched the armrests as if she feared being blown away.

"Maria wants to go home for Christmas," Bessie said to her son seated uncomfortably on a chair across from her in the living room.

"Just tell her she can't go."

"She'll quit."

"Then tell her you'll pay for an extra week, and you can come to us for the holidays."

"No. You'll all be running off in different directions and your home will be crazier than ever. There isn't even a calm time when the family can sit down and eat together. But, I guess that's not necessary. You can stand up and eat pizza.

You will be working and the kids have their own friends with things to do. That will leave Barbara."

"Don't be silly. Barbara would be happy to have you stay with us."

"Leonard, there is no sense pretending. We both know that your wife and I don't have the same values in life. We are polite to one another, but that's it. There is no love lost between us. Now that the kids are older and are off on their own, Barbara has the freedom she needs to pursue her commercial talents. She shops!"

"So I'll tell her to stop shopping for a week. I'll save a few dollars."

"You will lose money on the divorce lawyers."

"Come on, Mother, don't be stubborn."

"No, I'll be in the way. I can't come to you."

"How about Fran? You could go visit her in Florida."

"At eighty-five, you don't go jumping on a plane. It could snow or the flight could be delayed. It's just too much. Oh yes, Fran sent me some fruit, grapefruit. I never eat grapefruit. You'll have to take them."

"Who sent the fruit?"

"Fran did." Bessie was annoyed she had to repeat herself. There was nothing wrong with his ears; he just didn't care.

"That's nice. When are they coming home? And what's wrong with Morris?"

"Don't you ever talk to your sister? He's got gout."

"He always gets gout. He should lay off all that rich food. Wouldn't hurt if he drank less beer. Mama you've got to eat more. You are skin and bones."

"Maria can't cook. Her food is terrible. It all tastes Spanish."

"Well teach her how to cook, then."

"I tried a thousand times. It doesn't help. Spanish hands make Spanish foods."

"She's not Spanish.  She's Puerto Rican."

"Rican, *schmeeken.* It's the same thing."

"How can Jewish dishes come out tasting Puerto Rican?"

"She sneaks in spices. She says she doesn't. I know she puts them in."

Leonard untwined his fingers and twirled his thumbs. Bessie saw him look at the clock, waiting for the minute he could leave. He'd been in the apartment for ten minutes. In another ten, he'd be gone. Bessie could time his visits to the second. In and out. Twenty minutes. It never varied. Leonard interrupted her thoughts.

"So what do you want me to do, call the agency for someone else? A temp to stay with you during the holidays?"

Bessie considered the nuisance it would be getting used to another woman. "No, it's too late to find anyone else."

The swinging door to the kitchen exploded open as Maria gave it a bang with her foot. She bustled into the living room carrying a tray with two cups of tea and a plate of cookies. Even from a distance, the cookies looked stale.

"Hello, Meester Abrams." Maria smiled, showing her gold front teeth. Her black hair hung in frizzled ringlets. Sturdy and squat, she had the legs of a sumo wrestler.

"It's Doctor Abrams," Bessie corrected. "It's 'doctor,' not 'Meester,' remember?"

Unperturbed, Maria continued to smile. "Hello, Dr. Abrams. How are you today?"

"I'm very fine. Thank you for asking."

Maria set the tray table beside Bessie and handed Leonard his cup of tea.

"Want a cookie, Doctor? They very good. They called Nabisco." Maria turned toward Bessie.

"Eat some cookies," Maria urged, as she handed Bessie her tea. "Eat, Missus You need to eat. You are so skinny."

"I'll eat when it's good.

Marie turned back to Leonard. "You doctor, you tell her eat. Maybe she dies if she don't eat .You think so?"

"Where are you going for Christmas, Maria? Mama tells me you want to take a week off." Leonard dunked his cookie in the tea to soften it.

"Home, I go home to the Bronx. I just be with my whole family. They are so many people now. We gonna have a big deal Christmas. I want to help my children cook, clean up the house, and buy presents for all of them." Maria smiled. Her gold tooth winked at Leonard.

Leonard smiled back, almost beginning to be amused by her

"We have a problem, Maria. Mama doesn't want to stay

at my house when you leave here. She will not go to my sister's house in Florida. Do you anyone who could stay with her while you are gone?"

Maria flushed hot. Bessie could tell from the woman's expression she was afraid of losing her job.

"No problem, Meester, I mean, Dr. Abrams. She will come to me. To my place in the Bronx. There is plenty room there. We take care of her. No problem."

Bessie glowered at Maria from eyelids layered like a folded fan. She spoke to Leonard in rapid Yiddish.

"Do you think I'm *meshugana*? (Do you think I'm crazy?) Do you imagine I can go there with all the cockroaches?

Maria swirled on her tank legs. "Cockroaches? I no have cockroaches."

She bolted from the room, tossing her head in a haughty swish.

Leonard sat wordless for a moment. "Well, you don't have to worry now about Maria, Mama. She'll quit anyway."

"She won't quit. She doesn't understand Yiddish."

"Why couldn't you have said '*voncin*'?" (bedbug)

"A cockroach is a cockroach in any language!"

"A *voncin* is not a cockroach! I'm not going to argue Yiddish with you. I have to go. I haven't even made hospital rounds yet. So, will you be going to Maria's or not?"

"Yes, I am going."

Leonard rolled his eyes toward the ceiling, and heaved a great sigh.

"Go, go! *Gai Gezunterhait!* (Go in health.)

Bessie glanced at the clock on the mantel. The allotted twenty minutes had actually passed. Leonard had stayed another eight minutes.

Bessie felt sad. If only there was a way she could tell him he didn't have to visit her at all. She listened for the front door to close after him.

When the door clicked shut, Bessie grabbed a cookie and began nibbling around the chocolate striped circle like a rat attacking an Edam cheese. Brushing every cookie crumb from her floral dress, Bessie stood, rising to her full height of four feet eight inches. She cocked her ear for noises from the kitchen.

Quickly, she flung her skinny, sagging-arms above her head, bending her body left and right ten times. She moved her arms and placed her hands at her waist and began doing a series of knee bends. Moving quickly, Bessie changed her position. She touched her Reeboks with her fingers three times before placing her palms against the carpet, her veined legs like two branches behind her body. Four pushups: not a grunt, not a growl, not a groan. She pulled herself up from the floor using the chair for assistance.

With due diligence, she pivoted, held the back of the armchair and, as graceful as a ballerina, Bessie extended one leg backward, her body rigid with a leg extension worthy of Pavlova. She ended her performance with her right arm lifted outward from her body, her hand gracefully held in a heart-throbbing curve, three fingers curled just so!

Slightly winded, Bessie plopped herself back to safety in her chair, reached down and pulled her knitting from a canvas bag near her feet. With a lackluster expression she began knitting, quickly clicking away on a pink angora sweater.

Sunday morning, Maria answered the doorbell at Bessie's apartment: "Good morning Dr. Abrams. We are ready here."

"That's good Maria. Where is Mama?"

"In her bedroom. She say she wants you to come and help her. She no want me."

Bessie sat on the edge of her bed, legs dangling.

"Ah, you're on time."

"Mama, are you ready?"

"Not so fast. Don't rush me. What do you think, that I have to go rushing off to Maria's place to see the roaches? Believe me, they'll wait."

"For God's sake, Mama. You're the one who said you wanted to go to Maria's. You can still change your mind and come to my house."

Bessie could hear his impatience and ignored it.

"Here, I want you to put this jewelry in your safe deposit box." She handed him a well-worn suede sack tied with a leather thong. "Don't take this home with you. Who knows what would happen to it at your house."

"Really? I didn't know you had such valuable jewelry."

"You don't know everything. It wasn't easy getting, believe me. I got. I got."

Like immigrants on the move, Leonard carried Bessie's heavy suitcase and makeup box. Maria toted two bags of groceries. Bessie insisted on carrying her adders-tongue fern in a ceramic pot. She stopped several times to catch her breath as they trudged downward

They managed to load the car, taking Bessie's plant first, squeezing it between the front seat and the back next to Maria. After loading everything else in the trunk, Leonard seated Bessie in the front.

Bessie was quiet. Leonard was hoping she would change her mind.

Bessie said nothing.

By some miracle, there was a parking place in front of Maria's building. Bessie stoically waited for Leonard to come around and open her door. She stared at the wall Opposite the car was a wall filled with wild graffiti. A red-as-blood door in the middle of the wall burst open and two young boys raced out.

One of them bumped into Leonard as he bent to open the trunk.

"Hey kid, watch it!"

"Screw you," the kid answered back, his brown eyes flashing.

The other boy peered into the front seat. "Hey, Grandma's home." He called to his brother, who now ran slowly toward them .

Maria beamed at the boy, "That's my grandson. My Carlos. Get Angelo, honey. He can help carry these things upstairs."

"Oh my God," Leonard moaned as he extricated Bessie from the car. "I wonder how many more of them are upstairs. You won't survive it, Mama."

"I'm a survivor. It's in my blood," she answered.

Leonard counted nineteen stairs as he looked up to the first landing, and prayed it was Maria's apartment.

"Are you alright, Mama?" he asked.

"Don't talk," she panted. She leaned against the wall. "You shouldn't talk while you're mountain climbing."

Her breathing became ragged She took in air in small gasps. A door opened at the top landing and the sound of voices floated down the stairway.

"Is that you, *Madre*?" A woman's voice called down from the open doorway above.

Maria smiled. "That's my daughter, Merta," Maria announced to Leonard and Bessie. She has Juanito, two boys, and a baby girl. You know, the pretty baby I told you about."

Bessie couldn't even manage a nod.

"They are waiting for us. I told them you would be here for lunch. Rita is cooking something special. She is the wife of my son, Roberto. She is a good cook, almost like me."

"*Oy vey*," Bessie murmured under her breath.

They had reached the top landing. The mixed aroma of onions, garlic, and some unknown spices wafted out from the open door.

"If this wasn't so tragic, it could be a comedy," Leonard mumbled.

Maria stood to one side of the door and waved Bessie inside as if announcing the Messiah. Bessie drew in a deep breath, held her shoulders back and her head high as she walked regally into the apartment. Maria's large family sat around the living room.

When Bessie entered, everyone stood. A few of the mothers or aunts or whoever they were reached down and pulled up a child to a standing position. Maria hurried from one family member to the next and announced to Bessie their names and rank in this family society.

As Maria came to end of the line, she suddenly looked upset.

"Where is Francisco? I would expect my husband to be here to greet us."

"He went to pick up the wine," Merta told her. "He will be right back."

Bessie went from person to person, trying to fix their names to their faces. She wondered why they all seemed so accepting of her being there. But it felt wonderful.

She slowly turned to Leonard and smiled.

"You can go now, son. I am sure everything will be hunky dory." She walked up to Leonard and kissed his cheek. "Don't worry, and thank you for bringing me here. I think I might be needed."

Touching the place on his cheek where his mother kissed him, Leonard backed toward the door. "Call me if you need me," he called to Maria, Merta, Juanita, Manuel, Roberto, Jesus, Carlos, Angelo, and anybody else who cared to listen. He turned quickly and walked out the door. As he stepped on the landing, he saw a huge amber-colored, multi-legged insect dart across the threshold into Maria's apartment.

# Anyone for Pinochle?
## Hal Peters

My two years of active duty in the U.S Coast Guard were near termination on that late day in April, and I was home on a day's liberty from my billet at Government Island in Alameda, California. The phone rang, and it was my longtime friend, Les. He'd recently married a wonderful blue-eyed blonde, Sandy, and they were living in an apartment in the area of San Rafael named for Bret Harte, the author who had once resided there. We hadn't spent much time together, because my former female companion was attending Stanford, and thus our dates were either in the South Bay or in Davis, her home. In November of that year, I terminated that two-year relationship and had not dated seriously since the breakup.

The reason for the call was to ask if I was available to fill in as a fourth for a pinochle game they'd planned for that afternoon. They suggested I bring my swim trunks, as it was a warm day, and the apartment complex had a pool. Sandy was also providing dinner. Since I had nothing planned, I answered affirmatively and headed over about 2:00 p.m. in my '55 Chevy.

Upon arriving, I was introduced to the other quarter of the pinochle foursome, whom I'd never met before. Her name was Renee, and she and Sandy were best friends from their days at San Rafael High School.

Admittedly, my first impression of this girl was somewhat blasé, She was attractive and well-spoken, obviously mature and intelligent, but her skin was leper-like! Seems the previous weekend she'd been sailing on San Francisco Bay and had received a severe sunburn. Thus, every inch of her nicely-formed body was peeling! A fact hard to conceal in a swimsuit.

However, as the afternoon turned to evening, and the two of us became more familiar, I realized this twenty-year-old had all the qualifications I'd hoped for in a lifelong companion. She was going through some tough times regarding family and she and her sister were doing their best financially, both working in San Francisco and living quite frugally. I took her home that evening and we talked further. I said I'd like to see her again and she didn't object.

The following morning at breakfast, I confidently announced to my mother that last night I met the girl that I wanted to marry. Upon further discussion, Mom explained that I should have remembered Renee, as we had given her and her sister rides home from Sunday school years before. Mother also knew Renee's parents. I reminded Mom that I'd have been between the ages of twelve and sixteen, and since Renee was four years my junior, there had been no reason for attraction for either of us.

We continued to date that spring and on July 10, 1958, I asked her to marry me. A beautiful diamond engagement ring was polished from a ring that was my dad's father's. There had nearly not been a ring at all, as Grandpa Henry, sipping a cocktail while floating on an inner-tube in a slough off the Sacramento River and paddling with his other hand and in the cold water, felt the ring slide off his finger and fall to the muddy bottom. My grandfather couldn't swim a stroke but the old saying, "Necessity is the mother of invention," surely applied, and in an instant, he slipped off the inner-tube, took a deep breath and kicked his way to the extremely muddy bottom. Visibility being impossible, he merely grabbed a handful of the mud, and returned to the surface, gasping. Voila! He opened his hand and there was the ring!

Fortunately, since that day there have been no similar mishaps, and Renee still proudly wears the stone.

Our sermon was postponed until after my discharge from the service on October 3, 1958. Nine days later, we were married in Reno at the "little Chapel," with our mothers and five others in attendance. That was nearly fifty-six years ago. I must confess that I frequently ask myself why this truly beautiful girl chose to marry me. No matter what the reason, I'm grateful every day of my life that she made that decision!

# The Varenna Prune Saga
Elisabeth Levy

Varenna has a problem: the breakfast buffet table is without prunes. What happened? Elisabeth complains. She is told that prunes are just not available. She doesn't believe it, writes an e-mail to the Dining Committee Chairman just before the committee meeting. The issue is not addressed, but budget cuts are mentioned.

She gets mad and writes a comment card: "**R**umor has it that due to budget cuts, no prunes will be available." The next day she gets an e-mail telling her the issue was discussed after the meeting and the stewed prunes are on backorder. She feels bad about the comment card.

Soon she gets a phone call from the chef's assistant. His feelings are hurt, and the shortage of prunes has nothing to do with budget cuts. Meanwhile, Elisabeth, still feeling remorseful, has a glorious idea. She tells the assistant to look at the comment card carefully, cross out the "**R**" and replace it with an "**H**". The assistant gets it and laughs.

A few days later, Elisabeth gets another e-mail. Varenna has checked all the suppliers, and in the foreseeable future there are no stewed prunes available. Now a light goes on in Elisabeth's head: She answers, pointing out that dried pitted prunes are readily available and she was under the assumption that Varenna buys dried pitted prunes and stews them on the premises. She hadn't thought stewed prunes must mean cooked prunes selling in jars or cans.

The crowning glory is her receiving a package with dried pitted prunes from a concerned friend. She runs into the chairman and says: "The prune business is alive and well. I even received a package of dried prunes from the State of Washington. Why can't you just serve dried prunes if you cannot stew them here?" His answer: "That's a good idea."

Only a few days after Elisabeth is told there are no prunes available anywhere, beautiful stewed prunes crown the breakfast buffet. In the meantime, her spies are checking the stores for jars of cooked prunes, and one Sunday morning, a jar with stewed prunes ready to eat is deposited in front of her apartment.

One question remains: Where does Varenna find them, or do they stew them here?

# Cleaning the Barn
Sally Tilbury

We bought our country property in 1989. Down the hill, near the fence, was a 1940s Quonset hut. We capitalize "Quonset" because it was named for the British engineer who designed it. These metal structures came into being because of the need to store equipment and house military personnel during World War II. They became mess halls and offices. Servicemen lived in them and servicemen's wives kept house in them—a dubious first nest. When these structures became available as War Surplus, farmers bought them for storage barns. Our Quonset hut gave us 100 feet of leaky storage space. Quonset huts, now over 70 years old, still usable, can be seen dotted throughout Sonoma County, interesting leftovers from World War II.

Prior to Mother's Day, an e-mail was launched from this house to our three daughters, their husbands, and children. It announced, "This year's Mother's Day celebration will include a cleaning of the Quonset hut. Wear your old gloves and watch for black widow spiders."

Sure enough, my family turned up in their work clothes. I had taken one look into the interior chasm of the dark and clammy Quonset hut before they arrived. It looked like Kmart gone bad. A commercial dumpster was positioned at the rear door. The threat was, "Anything you do not take away will be thrown away." Each of us came into this world without even a pair of socks, but oh! the junk we have accumulated over a lifetime to cover our nakedness.

When you live in the country, there are absolutes. There will be dogs. Your friends and relatives give them to you because the poor creatures will be happier in the country. They come with names. Consequently, we have had two dropouts from the Guide Dogs for the Blind organization in Los Angeles and our present golden retriever, a rescue dog the organization found tied to a tree. Another absolute is that your barn storage will be used. Friends and relatives are pleased to store all the flotsam and jetsam of their lives. They may say, "May we store our son's car in your Quonset hut while he is gone? Are his skis still there? Someday we will come for all his stuff." They *ha ha* and we smile with a slight *grrr*. Clearly, the way to rid oneself of "stuff" is to give it to someone else.

We first stored a 1971 Chevrolet truck. After his father died, our friend decided the Quonset hut would be a good place to store his dad's truck. Someday our friend would need it. Of course. We understood. That truck still made it to and from the dump and we and our neighbors used it for hauling manure, gravel for potholes on the road we shared, bags of cement, nursery stock. On this Mother's Day, it was still used, insured, and appreciated. It held itself together with gratitude for a place to sleep. If a ranch truck needed to be needed, this was the place. It belonged to the neighborhood.

Among the junk in the Quonset hut were rusty bicycles, tired gym equipment, a spare tire, material from the Community Council, and the signs advertising the Crafts Fair The word "clutter" does not apply. This structure had become a home for colossal junk. A regular, self-respecting attic would not store these items.

I opened one cardboard box. It contained four Haviland cups that belonged to the saucers I unearthed in another container. We could have tea right here. Auntie Alice died and bequeathed her boxes of junk to Auntie Peg. Auntie Peg died and left her combined junk to Chuck's mother. Chuck's mother left her home and moved to a retirement facility. A dutiful son, my husband said, "Don't worry, Mom. We'll store it."

These British sisters had taste that ran from Spode and Wedgwood to the category known as "American Dime Store." Tchotchkes among the Chippendale. Among the stored items were four cardboard boxes of undated photos of nameless people, photos of fetching fat babies and on to World War I soldiers, dapper and proud on their way to the Front, followed by photos of flirty flappers in provocative poses. By default, I inherited these artifacts when Chuck passed. It must be some sort of revenge.

In the Quonset hut were non-functioning lamps and a tangled telephone instrument. I was ruthless. Out with it! The leaky aluminum canoe held tools and dried paint cans, rolls of deer fencing, rope, posts and chicken wire, items without which you cannot run your life. But would I throw out an old wooden dog bed? Not a chance. It would be like throwing out the crib.

One son-in-law said, "You mean you still have those old bicycles?" Was he crazy? Would this child of the Great Depression throw out a worn bicycle with petrified rubber tires? Never. It would be up to them. "Someday has arrived," I reminded him.

One of our daughters and her husband came away from a cardboard box with that look that comes from looking at old school papers. It is like falling in love again. Others smiled fondly at the old gas range from their first home and a full three-drawer filing cabinet filled with Lester's law school papers. Mary found a photo she had taken of the Twin Towers when she worked in New York. We gathered to remember.

While they spent time all dewy-eyed over precious papers, I urged them on toward the aluminum canoe. The canoe issue was complex. One of our young employees asked if he could store it. He had gotten a deal. Oh, he would patch the aluminum someday and we could all share in the joy of paddling the oversized canoe on the Russian River. That was 23 years ago. I think he switched to girls before someday came. The children all felt the canoe with the holes in it should be patched and put into the irrigation pond. But I have grown old waiting for things to be fixed. I did not intend to create a Yuppie still life down the hill on the dock with an upside-down canoe, so the canoe was positioned in the Salvation Army pile. They could melt it down. Think of the tambourines it might make.

After that fateful Mother's Day, the only things remaining were the ample woodpile and the green truck. Now that the Quonset hut is all cleaned out and hosed down, perhaps the grandchildren will find another homeless puppy for me. After all, I have the dog bed. They threaten, but I have learned to say, "No."

Yet, there is always someday.

# My Bali Hai Experience
## Nancy Humphriss

The trip from L.A. to Samoa was long, so I hoped fate would spare me and not seat me next to a restless two-year-old or a very large person who'd spill over into my already narrow tourist space. As luck would have it, my seatmate turned out to be a young, slender woman who was to be my first link in a serendipitous long weekend. Gail was from Vancouver, twenty-three, a bank teller eager to flee her humdrum life and spread her wings. She had saved what she could from her meager salary, and with the help of her supportive parents, bought a round-the-world ticket. The first stop on her journey was, as was mine, Samoa. I, on the other hand, was headed for Sydney to join Dale, who was working there.

It was 1980, and I was eager to start our new life. However, since my ticket allowed me to stop anywhere en route, I was looking forward to an adventure of my own in Pago Pago. Just the name of the city sounded exotic and exciting to me! I had done my travel homework before leaving, not willing to trust completely to chance, and therefore had booked a reservation in the only hotel on the island. Fate had given me the last room available. During the flight, Gail asked me where I planned to stay. I replied, "*The Rainmaker.* It's the only hotel in Pago Pago. I hope you've made a reservation there."

She replied that she hadn't, and maybe she had made a mistake, not realizing there weren't many places to stay. Being a nice person, and feeling Gail was, too, I found myself asking her to stay with me if the room had two beds. She quickly accepted my offer, and we talked on about what might lie ahead in Samoa.

We arrived at the Samoan airport, which turned out to be a small thatched-roof building, with one Samoan manning the passport check and one dragging luggage out of the plane. I looked around for a taxi stand or bus information, but there was none to be had. Asking the man at the desk about transportation into the city, he said it was up to me. No taxis were available, but if I stood at the side of the road in front of the airport, sooner or later, someone driving by would stop and give me a ride, for a small charge, of course. The narrow road had no stores, buildings, or even houses, and looked very lonely and desolate. But Gail and I did as the man suggested, and after several cars drove by, one stopped. The driver suggested a small fee, and we heaved our suitcases in the tiny trunk, jumped into the back seat, and prepared to leave.

Before the driver could get started, a young man came running full speed out of the airport, waving his hands. Obviously, he hoped to get a ride in the front seat, so the driver waited until he got in, his small bag on his lap, and off we went. The drive into Pago Pago took about 20 minutes, and at one point, the young man introduced himself as Tony from Perth, Australia. He had been backpacking for fourteen months, and now was on his last stop before home and a job. "Where are you staying?" he asked.

"*The Rainmaker*," replied Gail. "We have the last room, and there are no other places available."

A few minutes of silence followed. Gail nudged me and whispered, "Why don't we invite him to stay with us?" At first I was hesitant, but I decided to live a little, and asked him to join us. He quickly agreed, and our fate was sealed.

Thus destiny initiated three of the most exciting, fun, free-style days I had ever had! The three of us checked into a hotel that seemed like something out of a Humphrey Bogart movie. Situated on the shore of the bay, volcanic mountains rising right up from the shoreline, this thatched-roofed hotel had a bar with a slowly twirling ceiling fan, which kept the air moving. Since there was little to do on the island, the guests and natives spent much of their time here, telling stories, interacting, enjoying life. After settling into our room with twin beds and a rollaway, we went into the bar for cocktails, where we were quickly joined by others, Samoans and tourists alike.

One particularly friendly native latched onto us, suggesting things to see and places to go. Samoa was a study in beauty and ugliness. Unfortunately, the town, not big enough to be called a city, was littered with beer cans, plastic bags, paper, and discarded junk. But outside the town, the island was really a tropical paradise, and I thought I was in Bali Hai.

One of the few days we were there, our Samoan friend took us to the village where he lived. His house was on a platform, with a thatched roof, of course, and one big room on stilts to keep it above ground. Several families lived there, sharing food, work, and often each other. Sex was considered to be just another bodily need like food and water. Natives watched out for each other, and food, goods, etc. were communally shared.

The Samoans are supposed to be among the last full-blooded Polynesians, and they are very concerned that they may end up like the Hawaiians with mixed blood. Therefore, they have very strict marriage laws, and no Samoan can marry a non-Samoan and remain on the island. They are very handsome people, happy, pleasant, relaxed. The saying, "If it feels good, do it," had to originate here. Life was easy, since food grew without effort, and money was needed for very little. The local market sold fruits and vegetables of all kinds, and women wove baskets of palm leaves to use for carrying groceries.

We wanted to buy some bananas, but the only way we could was by buying the whole stalk—about thirty bananas!

One day, our self-appointed guide took us to a school, and there was an art show in progress. The designs were painted on tree bark, flattened and smoothed out. Many were quite lovely, and I wanted to buy one or two to take with me. Much to my surprise, while they were for sale at an incredibly low price, I was not allowed to buy one. The reason? They wanted the art work to stay on the island and not become simply tourist merchandise. I had never encountered a place where money held so little interest!

Our last evening there, we sipped our wine outside on a balcony while Tony gave us lessons on the stars in the Southern Hemisphere. He pointed out the Southern Cross and other constellations I had never seen. A magical, celestial sight! The tropical smells, the swaying palms, the warm companions, all seemed to send up a heady, romantic aura of suspended time.

In the lounge where we sat for the final time, a handsome Samoan decided he wanted Gail, but she became mute with fear, since he was not shy and a bit aggressive. When she showed no response to his advances, he decided I would be his second choice. I had some anxious moments, but Tony prevailed and the native disappeared. We went into the dining room and sat down for dinner. Who should appear and sit down with us but our Samoan lover! Uninvited, of course! He ordered his dinner, and when he obviously was being ignored, he left. But before doing so, he put his empty plate under the table. Why? He was skipping the bill! The waiter, also Samoan, said he did this fairly often and was only mildly annoyed. He didn't pay for his meal, nor did we, and no one seemed at all concerned.

The next morning Tony and Gail decided to take the eight-hour ferry ride to Western Samoa, supposedly beautiful and even more unspoiled than American Samoa. I walked to the dock with them, and watched them sadly as they sailed away. Oh, how I wished I could go along, but Sydney, Dale, and an exciting life awaited me. I speculated on what destiny had in store for them on the exciting threshold of life, and I hoped fate would be good to them. At this moment, I realized how lucky I had been that our paths crossed in this serendipitous way. I wouldn't have missed this enchanting interlude for anything. Was this a lucky encounter, my fate, my destiny, or just a brief coincidence in my life? Whatever the answer, I am grateful for the lovely memory.

# Four Haiku
Joyce Cass

raindrops spilling down my windshield
somewhere
soldiers' mothers' tears are mine


pebbles of unrest
are not washed away
by forces of the main stream


something is sharing
my morning muffin
a mousie in the pantry?


summer pleasures
ice tinkling in glass
cool contemplation of navel

# Happiness
## Shirley Johnson

It was a mild sunny day in early May in Claremont, California. I was sitting on the floor of our house in front of the sliding glass doors that opened on a small, pleasant, grassy space that would someday become a garden. A hummingbird darted in front of the door, aiming perfectly at the nectar in a fuscia that hung in a basket outside. Only my three-month-old baby was with me in the house, quietly resting in my arms, at last at peace, letting me know after a bumpy start in life with few hours of sleep for either of us, that at last she liked it here in this world, in this place, with me, where she was safe. It was then I had a sudden, deep knowledge of happiness, and, best of all, I knew what that moment was and that I would carry it in my heart for the rest of my days.

# AUTHOR BIOS

**Leona Hansen Biddle** was a teenager when she emigrated from Odense, Denmark, in 1950. She earned her degree from the University of Idaho, and has lived in Portland, Seattle, and the Bay Area. She moved to Varenna in 2013 and joined the Writers Club soon after. She has long been a patron of the arts, serving on the Napa Valley and Santa Rosa Symphony Leagues, and helping to restore the Napa Valley Opera House. She enjoys painting, bridge, bocce, golf, writing, reading, cooking, entertaining, and life!

**Susan Bono, Editor,** is a writing teacher, freelance editor living in Petaluma. She edited and published *Tiny Lights: A Journal of Personal Narrative* and its online counterpart, www.tiny-lights.com, from 1995-2014. Her writing has appeared in publications such as Sheila Bender's *Writing & Publishing Personal Essays*, the *St. Petersburg Times*, the *Petaluma Argus Courier*, and *Passager Magazine*. Her book of collected essays, *What Have We Here: Essays about Keeping House and Finding Home*, is

**Joyce Cass** (1926-2014) was born in San Francisco, leaving her heart there. Through the years she lived at twenty different residences in Northern California, with the exception of two high school years spent at boarding school in Lake Forest, Illinois. Her four children all live in the Bay Area, with eight grand-girls and six great-grandchildren. Joyce delighted in being part of the Varenna Writers Club. She is missed.

**Karin R. Fitzgerald** was named Rose Karin after her German and Swedish grandmothers, and called "Rose" by her family. She knew at a very young age that "Rose" didn't fit her, but a given name is a lot like a porcupine quill: once embedded, it's hard to remove. She tried unsuccessfully to ditch the "Rose," but the name stayed with her like an unwanted house guest. Love solved the problem when student nurse Rose Karin met handsome law student James Martin Fitzgerald. For sixty-one years of marriage, darling James called her Karin, and so did everyone else.

**Dorothy Herbert** was born in Cleveland, Ohio, in 1924. Her childhood was split between Ohio and Southern California. She graduated from the University of California, Berkeley. This was followed by a year of training in laboratory technology at Western Reserve in Cleveland. Her career as a lab tech allowed her to spend two years in Dhahran, Saudi Arabia, and later, a year in Oxford, England, during her boss's sabbatical. After her retirement from UCSF, she happily settled in Sonoma and then Santa Rosa, California.

**Nancy Humphriss** grew up in the small town of Northampton, Massachusetts. After graduating from the University of Massachusetts, she married her hometown sweetheart, raised a family, and followed her husband to seven different states, Sydney, Australia, for four years, and one year in Jerusalem. Her teaching career began with first graders in Florida. After earning her Master's Degree in Comparative Literature from Indiana University, Nancy ended her career teaching foreign students for 17 years at San Jose State University. She and her husband retired to Santa Rosa in 1997, and moved to Varenna in 2009. She feels very fortunate to have had such a satisfying life.

**Shirley Johnson** studied Foreign Languages at the Universities of Minnesota and Wisconsin. After marrying and having three children, she taught Spanish in a California community college for some twenty years. While always a constant reader, she didn't write until she joined a memoir group while living in Carmel. Using materials from those memoirs, she put together the story of her life in a self-published book for her children and grandchildren. When she arrived among the first group of residents at Varenna, she was happy to find others with similar interests and joined the Writers Club.

**Nikki King** was born and raised in Fargo, North Dakota, and received her B.A. from Mills College in Oakland, California. After graduation, she moved to San Francisco where she married a student from USF Law School. She and her husband (now a retired Justice) have one son and have been married for 56 years. At age 49, she went back to graduate school, got a master's degree in Counseling, and was a psychotherapist for 11 years before retiring. In her retirement years at Varenna, Nikki has decided that this is the time to put down reflections on her life experiences and write brief memoirs about incidents that stand out in her mind.

Born in Chicago, **Judith Klausner** grew up in Glencoe, Illinois. She attended the University of Wisconsin as a modern dance major and received her BS degree in Art Therapy from the State University of New York. With acclaimed sculptor Hana Geber as a mentor, Judith continued to push the envelope of her work. She was greatly influenced by sabbaticals in Italy and Israel. In Israel, the spirit of the people, the desert, and the Bible became a focus for her work. In Florence, she designed and cast four bronze doors for a synagogue in New York. Judith is the author of three books and several short stories, including four in the *New York Times*.

**Elisabeth Levy** was born, raised and trained as a registered nurse in Switzerland. In 1958 she immigrated to the USA, working a few months in Portland, Oregon, Galveston and San Antonio, Texas, before settling in San Francisco, California. She worked in Dermatology with her husband, Dr. S. William Levy until he died in 2005. She always liked to write, and in 2006 started getting serious. She joined the Oakmont Writers and published *Destiny*, a translation of her friend's life as a paraplegic and several essays in the yearly Oakmont Writers Anthologies. She continues to play a vital role in supporting Varenna's writers.

**Hal Peters** spent his first eleven years in the Sacramento Valley as the son of a sheep rancher in a town with a population of 1,100. When his parents divorced, he and his mother moved to Marin County, where he lived until 1962. That's when he, his wife, and son settled in Orange County and he began his career as a manufacturer's agent for sporting goods and sportswear manufacturers. In 1990, he retired and lived in Monterey County until 2006, when he came to Santa Rosa. As a high school English major, he especially enjoyed essay composition and is delighted to reintroduce himself to the craft as a member of the Varenna Writers Club.

**Jack Russ** shifted his writing focus to fiction in 1999, after years of professional non-fiction. He earned awards for three short stories and published his first novel, *In Dangerous Waters*, in December 2010. For three years he served as President of the Mt. Diablo Branch of the California Writers Club, and concurrently formed and promoted the Tri-Valley Branch of CWC. Jack holds a MA in Management and is a retired Navy Captain and carrier pilot. He and his wife Arlene moved to Varenna in May 2011.

**Bernice Schachter** was born in Elizabeth, New Jersey, and lived in the town of Linden until she moved to Southern California in 1973. She earned a Master's Degree in Sculpture from Goddard College in Vermont, studied Art History at California State College in Northridge, and taught sculpture part-time at Everywoman's Village in Van Nys for twenty-five years. She spent summers in Pietrasanta, Italy, teaching the Italian method of stone carving. After retiring to Laguna Woods Village, Bernice found the time to write two books, *The Masks of My Muse* and *The Creative Quest*. She is currently working on *A Legacy in Stone* for her great-grandchildren who are yet to be.

**Floyd Schlosser** was a naval aviator for 25 years and a court divorce mediator for the succeeding 25 years. He developed an avid interest in the arts and theater and interacting with others having similar interests. He spent several years based in Italy enjoying that culture and other societies as well—especially the animated manner of expression in other Mediterranean cultures. Floyd is married to Ginger and they have a son residing in Alaska, where they enjoy visiting annually in the summer.

 **Sally Tilbury** and her husband worked in the family business prior to retirement. Beverly Hills Travel, Inc., a commercial travel agency, had five offices, with their flagship office in the Beverly Hills Hotel. She moved with her husband to Sonoma County in 1990, and upon her husband's death, she came to live at Varenna. She has three daughters, six grandchildren, and six great-grandchildren all living in Northern California.